PIGMALION'S REVERIE: A KOREAN'S MISREADING OF MAJOR AMERICAN AND BRITISH POETRY

PIGMALION'S REVERIE: A KOREAN'S MISREADING OF MAJOR AMERICAN AND BRITISH POETRY

Sharing Reading English Poetry with the Global Nomads

Kyu-myoung Lee

PARTRIDGE

To order additional copies of this book, contact
Toll Free 800 101 2657 (Singapore)
Toll Free 1 800 81 7340 (Malaysia)
orders.singapore@partridgepublishing.com

www.partridgepublishing.com/singapore

Dedicated to worldwide nomads
in search of truth of life

CONTENTS

A VIEW OF PROCRUSTES' BED

Readers might remember the mythic figure Procrustes, who would commit a first-class crime similar to what you might see in the movie *The Texas Chainsaw Massacre*. It is said that he would make a stranger's legs fit the length of a bed. This could be linked to the subjective position of things or humans or texts and may sound negative. I dare to confirm that this is the common point everybody practices all day long. It is why humans can see something concerning their interests or benefit or taste or aims from their own perspective.

Of course, an objective view also would not be different from a subjective view, since the former can be legislated by the latter. Thus, the Greek bed would correspond to the objective standard or criteria of a community, and Procrustes would correspond to the subjective enforcer. Likewise, although a poem remains in an objective state, readers wearing coloured eyeglasses are approaching it from a subjective viewpoint. The letters of the poem are the same to all readers, but their minds are separate. Their minds are coloured by diverse objective views: modernism, postmodernism, feminism, post-feminism, colonialism, and post-colonialism. Even Buddhism stresses that there would be no boundary between subjective and objective views.

Thus, arguing about how to read poems is fruitless. The positive or negative position on poetry as the primal genre of literature appeared in the Old Greek era. The representative scholars are Plato and Aristotle, among which the former, in his *Republic*, criticised poets because they might make the public stupid, helpless, and absentminded through vain rhetoric and pun, alienating them from reality. His theory of "idea" didn't recognise poets as the apostles of truth in that all things on Earth would be like only fakes as the copies deviated from the originals in the residence of truth, "idea."

On the other hand, Plato's pupil, Aristotle, stood on the opposite position; he recognized that tragedy as a part of poetics might have the function of healing people's emotions, as sympathizing with the tragic hero in the tragedy, releasing "pity and fear", feeling "catharsis", and resolving their frustration with their realities might be helpful in governing them.

Philip Sidney, in *An Apology for Poetry*, argued that poets do not imitate nature but can recreate nature and that poetry could benefit society, people, and governance. His opinion is plausible because poetry, in the form of oral songs, provides exhausted people suffering because of survival games or horrible realities linked to the diverse themes implicated in the affairs of humans, nature, and religion with a bit of consolation, comfort, cooperation, or exhortation, like the worldwide charity song "We Are the World."

In this book, we will examine the masterpieces of famous dead poets in the subjective or the objective view, in addition to cultural recognitions accompanying rather philosophical and literary terms. As there are no correct readings in the world, although close readings remain, most readings would be "misreadings", as suggested by the great American scholar Harold Bloom. Thus, readers have the inviolable privilege of enjoying reading poetry, and my sheer or foolish interpretations in this book can become practical examples of comic "misreadings", making you secrete endorphins (or dopamine or serotonin) for the benefit of your health.

Have you heard of the so-called Korean Wave, as it relates to Korean pop, drama, movies, cuisine, and fashion? I wonder if my book would be a juicy fruit or sour one, allowing the world's citizens either to appreciate or criticise this Oriental nomad's observations, which have been gained through existing in the "global village" rather than being confined in Korean society.

CHAPTER 1

JOHN DONNE: COMPLAINTS TO THE CREATOR

John Donne (1572–1631) reminds me of the dogmatic Franciscan friar William of Baskerville in the movie *The Name of the Rose* (based on the novel by Umberto Eco), who tried to grasp the ultimate truth of life from the gigantic archive of the monastery, in which many pious priests strove to transcribe and interpret the Bible. He resembles the lofty priest in that he pursued the metaphysical spirit in the then "black age", when witch trials took place in the open. One of these trials saw Joan of Arc accused of witchcraft and burned. In the era when Catholicism monopolised the goodwill of the human soul and the afterlife, his focus on a metaphysical poetics might have been at the risk of his life. In postmodern times, if he argued for the metaphysics J. Derrida hated, he must be blamed for being an anachronistic human. He favoured the reasonable, witty terms of "conceit" and "paradox", which would positively light that age of illiteracy and relieve the reading public of the bitter pains of the same inconvenient realities as primitive times. Although their physical lives were miserable, his witty poems consoled the reading people. On the other hand, his metapoetics triggered the motive that humans were more alienated from authoritative and despotic realities.

Donne was innately Roman Catholic because all his family had believed in Roman Catholicism. But that was contrary to the Anglican Church under the domain of Elizabeth I (1533–1603). Naturally, he suffered from the mutual persecution between the two similar religions. For the religious troubles of Britain, Mary, Queen of Scots (1542–87), who admired Catholicism, was beheaded, which caused Spain, the Catholic kingdom, to attack England. Ironically, her son, either James I (in England) or James VI (in Scotland), became the double king of Scotland and England because Queen Elizabeth I had had no son and James VI of Scotland occupied the throne of England.

In addition, he refused any degrees from Oxford and Cambridge, as the universities would force him to follow the tenets of Anglicanism. But in the end, his sincere belief in Catholicism succumbed to Anglicanism since his beloved brother had died from religious suppression. Thus, his poetry was full of complaints of religious ambiguity toward God and indications of the human tenacity to grasp the very secret of human genesis.

His marriage was chaotic and uneven. Donne was accused of a "disapproved event" with a daughter of higher nobility and briefly imprisoned, so that he didn't receive any dowry. Themes such as secular marriage and love affairs rising from this domestic happening were sublimated into his poetry. As the rich father-in-law discarded him, Donne suffered bitter poverty resulting from his many dependents, especially his twelve children, until he was employed as royal chaplain (today public pastor) at the cost of flattering the king, perhaps to escape from a financial crisis, although he sarcastically accused humans of duplicity in his main themes.

The title of his masterpiece "The Good-Morrow" implicates the temporality of life, as seen in the short, brisk period of "morrow" compared with the boring eternity of God. Although humans live in a blinking moment, should they love a true love?

> I wonder by my troth, what thou and I
> Did, till we loved? Were we not wean'd till then?
> But suck'd on country pleasures, childishly?
> Or snorted we in the Seven Sleepers' den?
> 'Twas so; but this, all pleasures fancies be;
> If ever any beauty I did see,
> Which I desired, and got, 'twas but a dream of thee.

> And now good-morrow to our waking souls,
> Which watch not one another out of fear;
> For love, all love of other sights controls,
> And makes one little room an everywhere.
> Let sea-discoverers to new worlds have gone,
> Let maps to other, worlds on worlds have shown,
> Let us possess one world, each hath one, and is one.

> My face in thine eye, thine in mine appears,
> And true plain hearts do in the faces rest;

Where can we find two better hemispheres,
Without sharp north, without declining west?
Whatever dies, was not mixed equally;
If our two loves be one, or, thou and I
Love so alike, that none do slacken, none can die.

Here, Hebraism and Hellenism are suggested, since "pleasures", which sinful humans enjoy, and pious "Seven Sleepers" in Ephesus that give up "pleasures" coexist. And given that the situations of the stanza can be applied to the Bible, scholasticism of the duet of rebirth and death, hope and despair emerge that we can hear vividly. All pleasures humans enjoy stay skin-deep and fleeting since even "any beauty" we ever encountered as a vitamin during our tedious lifetimes may be equal to "dream" or "fancies." Thus, trying to chase erotic, gorgeous "pleasures" would be childish, like dreaming of a fairy tale.

In the sunny morning, why can't sensible, mature lovers watch each other out of "fear"? That would be why morning quickly goes away, like the golden chariot of Pharaoh chasing Moses. This reminds me of an epigram of Buddhism: Don't meet each other; this preconditions "parting" in the future perfect view. Also, "fear" would be caused by ephemeral human fate, including the oppositions of others, such as parents, other relatives, and acquaintances. True love is more worthy than any other beautiful, impressive sight.

By the way, what does "makes one little room an everywhere" connote? It is paralleled with the fantasy that the moon and stars everywhere shine and bless only the lovers falling into self-referential or imaginary views. Then holism is suggested as one-plus-one equals not two but rather one. A whole can be born from a part-plus-part so it can function as an animated device, such as car, ship, aeroplane, family, or company.

> My face in thine eye, thine in mine appears,
> And true plain hearts do in the faces rest;
> Where can we find two better hemispheres
> Without sharp north, without declining west?
> Whatever dies, was not mix'd equally;
> If our two loves be one, or thou and I
> Love so alike that none can slacken, none can die.

This part shows us altruism as the identified relation between "mine" and "thine". "True plain hearts" symbolise the hopeful model of humanity the narrator wishes for without the contrary sides such as "north" and "west". He reasons that human death would be due to the imbalance of the opposite sides, as the weak side is attracted to the strong side. Likewise, it is attracted to the stronger side, like a biased, comparative circulation or shift of power, and linked to the "middle path" (中道) between the physical and spiritual sides that Buddha focused on as the key virtue of spiritual awakening. Without differences in our lives, it is common to think of ourselves as the world or become the whole or "one" without boundaries, envies, conflicts, and wars. In this sense, "worlds on worlds" would be a kind of earthly paradise in which equality is completely embodied. If the mass of love between humans were equal, how can ferocious slaughter happen, as seen in today's internecine situations? But as the world is composed of materials waxing and waning, the narrator's ideal can't be realised on Earth at all, because carnivorous lions should feed on rabbits, and humans loyal to the "principle of pleasure" will still strive to desire material and spiritual well-being.

I think this poem may not simply be a love poem but one that mordantly points to contradictions, or different phenomena, as the causes of conflicts regarding all things in the world. To overcome this tragic situation, humans should become "one" rather than one-time political campaigners. This shows us the poet's profound humanitarianism, declaring that human spirituality, blind and subject to various religions amid illiteracy, might have bidden a farewell to the Dark Age.

The next poem for us to read is "Holy Sonnet: Batter My Heart, Three-Person'd God", which implicates the absurd, irreversible relation between the Holy Creator and humble creatures. Notwithstanding, despite sending many complaints to the Creator, humans can't be paralleled with the Creator. Besides the essence of the universe only God knows, the Maker allows impolite humans, challenging divinity, to be at the disposal of the superficial knowledge of its crust. Through this, they become more advanced in their daily routines.

Batter my heart, three-person'd God, for you
As yet but knock, breathe, shine, and seek to mend;

That I may rise and stand, o'erthrow me, and bend
Your force to break, blow, burn, and make me new.

For this part, my answer to Donne, though miserable
and stuffy, is as follows. If humans were perfect beings,
they would not be humans. They were born with flaws
lethal to life, so they should strive to fix them despite the
worst weather of resistance and defence. Figuratively,
humans have the confirmed, miserable fate to head for
each self-referential paradise on the earth or in the sky,
as a ferryman should drain water permeating the ferry.
Humans are surrounded by inner and outer enemies,
such as the neurosis arising from the discontent between
an ideal and its fruits, as well as competitive others,
such as foes and fatal wounds, to death caused from
formidable elements such as tornados and tsunamis.
They are cornered with all sorts of critical situations
about which Hamlet also agonised. This can remind us
of the masochistic life of feeling a momentary euphoria,
such as a transient happiness after a tiring labour, which
can be recognised as the most contradictory, worst
conditions of humans. In this sense, as humans do not
know both the aim and cause of creation, they receive
the passive capacity of imagination nonsensically to infer
its essence or identity merely from the appearance of
something, as the blind feel an elephant and proclaim its
definition. Accordingly, human imagination functions
as a supplement of presence to appease and comfort
humans alienated from their origin, like babies cast from
the womb. If they knew the secrets of creation, what

would they do? The catastrophe can be inferred from the history of corrupt Catholic priests selling tickets to heaven before the Reformation Martin Luther triggered.

> I, like an usurp'd town to another due,
> Labor to admit you, but oh, to no end;
> Reason, your viceroy in me, me should defend,
> But is captiv'd, and proves weak or untrue.
> Yet dearly I love you, and would be lov'd fain,

The Creator forces humans to have "reason" as a kind of "super-ego", suggested by Dr. Freud. But "reason" can't stand by humans unlike their hopeful expectation and can't lead them to the Creator. By the way, if "reason" makes humans perfect, it would be not God's providence. Thus, humans fall into a dilemma. If humans "love" God, it is because they never do wrong. But despite "reason" as divine device given from God, they cannot help committing crimes and sins due to envy and greed as fundamental human characteristics, so all they can do is feel agonised and regretful for their faults. Of course, there are other stately, brazen humans who do not feel guilty, such as F. Nietzsche and K. Marx, despite violating God's providence prohibiting physical and spiritual faults. The reason humans can't help committing crimes is that they should live faced with antagonistic, contradictory relations: master and slave, employer and employee, government party and opposition party.

But am betroth'd unto your enemy;
Divorce me, untie or break that knot again,
Take me to you, imprison me, for I,
Except you enthrall me, never shall be free,
Nor ever chaste, except you ravish me.

Although humans received the amazing grace of creation and even "reason" as a guard agent from God, they have betrayed God and are even conspiring with Satan against God, like Dr Faust. Thus, the narrator doubting the power of reason rather wants to unconditionally resort to God's detention, heading for goodness, though boring and uninteresting, compared to the interesting, sweet tricks of Satan. Namely, if humans would not be occupied with God, as they were with Satan, the narrator had better stay under the guard or intervention of God as seen in the line "except you ravish me."

CHAPTER 2

J. KEATS: A CRUSADE FOR TRUTH

Keats has been regarded as among the best of the shimmering poets in English society. Of course, other Westerners would suggest their favourite poet to me—Hölderlin, Rimbaud, or Pushkin—whom I will read in future. The charms of his poetry can be simply summarised as pursuing the ultimate truth and relieving brutal realities. The deserving works out of his poetry are incalculable: a few of the "Odes" and "The Eve of St. Agnes." Among them, I will begin with "Ode to a Nightingale". Hanging about its surroundings in inner and outer ways, ironically I will grasp this or that shape of this poem only to misunderstand it in my own delusion according to Jacques Lacan's view that a recognition of a thing is no more than its misrecognition, which humans never evade at all. What shall I do? Notwithstanding, I can't help reading it, though detouring its core, which seems to be my destiny, simultaneously the destinies of all humans and Sisyphus with wearing blind glasses and seeming to look at lovers and repeating each boring job. I am writing and writing books out of habit, as a major-league pitcher is throwing and throwing balls for raking in money, and Bob Dylan, the laureate poet of the 2016 Nobel Prize, is singing and singing for ascending the altar of the Muse.

At first, I will try to read "Ode to a Nightingale" through system of code since we can never read the poem itself. Namely, we can recognise the poem only if it should yield to the linguistic system.

> MY heart aches, and a drowsy numbness pains
> My sense, as though of hemlock I had drunk,
> Or emptied some dull opiate to the drains
> One minute past, and Lethe-wards had sunk:
> 'Tis not through envy of thy happy lot, 5
> But being too happy in thine happiness,
> That thou, light-wingèd Dryad of the trees,
> In some melodious plot
> Of beechen green, and shadows numberless,
> Singest of summer in full-throated ease. 10

Here "Lethe" reminds me of the "principle of Thanatos" suggested by S. Freud, which means the cowardly instinct to escape from our ferocious realities fed and feeding, or to long for the maternity of relief from the battles of life with "my sense" numbed by otherness or regularisation. On the other hand, "thy happy lot" that the narrator envies can be linked to the misfortune of tongue-cut Philoméla, chased and castrated by birds of prey since, actually, the birds are under the umbrella of nature. Through the auditory image revealed in

"Singest of summer in full-throated ease," the narrator consoles readers exhausted from the tough realities. Of course, this can be the spellbound role of poetry that Plato criticised.

> O for a draught of vintage! that hath been
> Cool'd a long age in the deep-delvèd earth,
> Tasting of Flora and the country-green,
> Dance, and Provençal song, and sunburnt mirth!
> O for a beaker full of the warm South! 15
> Full of the true, the blushful Hippocrene,
> With beaded bubbles winking at the brim,
> And purple-stainèd mouth;
> That I might drink, and leave the world unseen,
> And with thee fade away into the forest dim: 20

The thirst for "vintage" as wine can be contrasted to the hunger for truth that we, like Godot, long for ambiguously, although existentialists have already declared no truth in the absurd world where Jesus functioning as the road and truth and life for our salvation stayed historically. When intoxicated in wine, residing in insanity would be beneficial for enduring the realities, as seen in "I might drink". Then the narrator would be in the company of the bird that would never attack him rather than among humans who would upset him. Accordingly, the thirst for wine would be seen as a yearning for the ideal world, free from the sensual sufferings in the world composed of materials resulting in combination and schism. This may mean that he

would forsake the physical power to overcome the world.
Namely, he would have resorted to the transcendental
consciousness of intoxicated numbness to face the terrible
sane world. What may be my purpose for existing in the
world? To drink wine or to eat bread or to work for a
job or date a girl or boy or write a book or hit a ball—
what to do else? Additionally, this part reminds us of the
impressive lines of Yeats' "The Lake Isle of Innisfree": I
will arise and go now, and go to Innisfree,/ And a small
cabin build there, of clay and wattles made:/ Nine bean-
rows will I have there, a hive for the honey-bee;/ And live
alone in the bee-loud glade." Thus, the "Nightingale" and
"Innisfree" can be paralleled to lead the narrators to the
ideal shelters to hide their worn egos.

> Fade far away, dissolve, and quite forget
> What thou among the leaves hast never known,
> The weariness, the fever, and the fret
> Here, where men sit and hear each other groan;
> Where palsy shakes a few, sad, last grey hairs, 25
> Where youth grows pale, and spectre-thin, and
> dies;
> Where but to think is to be full of sorrow
> And leaden-eyed despairs;
> Where beauty cannot keep her lustrous eyes,
> Or new Love pine at them beyond to-morrow. 30

The principle of the world suggested in the stanza
is that of "entropy" for all humans to be subject to. It
signifies the transformation of moving valuable things

to valueless things and happening in the brutal coliseum of sequential "where". The site is full of the unavoidable passages of birth, ageing, illness, and death, for which Buddha left his comfortable home and beloved family to search for the ultimate truth to survive the curse of "entropy". Moreover, Jesus came down here to the damned world, as denoted in "Where youth grows pale, and spectre-thin, and dies", to save sinful humans in the disguise of a plain carpenter despite being the subject of the big bang. As is often the case, humans regard temporary things such as money, beauty, fame, and work as eternal monuments, which is reflected in the lines "Where beauty cannot keep her lustrous eyes,/ Or new Love pine at them beyond to-morrow". Readers, how can humans as momentary beings expect "tomorrow"? It can be a phenomenal conceit. Namely, we are living in the desperate world where time murders things and water erodes the earth, dreaming of the tour to Mars or a quick-frozen, mummified state for eternity.

> Away! away! for I will fly to thee,
> Not charioted by Bacchus and his pards (leopards),
> But on the viewless wings of Poesy,
> Though the dull brain perplexes and retards:
> Already with thee! tender is the night, 35
> And haply the Queen-Moon is on her throne,
> Cluster'd around by all her starry Fays
> But here there is no light,
> Save what from heaven is with the breezes blown

Through verdurous glooms and winding mossy
ways. 40

The narrator is struggling to escape from the boring
realities, but s/he must recognize that we are physically
confined to our realities in which we are deployed
according to each role in the factory, office, field and
home as seen in the lines of the famed pop, "Hotel
California": "Mirrors on the ceiling, the pink champagne
on ice./ And she said "We are all just prisoners here, of
our own device./ ... "Relax," said the night man, "We
are programmed to receive./ You can check-out any
time you like but you can never leave." Symbolically,
we are given the titles of the sites fit for each mission,
so-called interpellation suggested by the famed French
socialist Althusser, which can be carved in each name
card and mind such as manager, boss, general, politician,
prosecutor, accountant, clerk, sergeant, professor,
engineer, poet, husband and wife, etc. The narrator tries
to decline the undeniable situations and head for his ideal
shelter, of all occasions, after undergoing several physical
barriers and surroundings such as "night", "moon",
"star", "breezes", "woods", and "ways." This would be a
contradictory but recognisable situation since humans
always tend to fly to a noble utopia where "Bacchus" and
his leopards may stay from the slovenly realities where
the foolish "Poesy" out of "the dull brain" resides. Thus,
our dystopia has no "light" to reflect the ultimate truth
of life and death but blurred "Poesy" of enlightenment,

which would be the "light" without "light", like the
fact without fact. But that this "Poesy" can please and
comfort absurd humans as prisoners confined to the
earth is a tragic comedy.

> I cannot see what flowers are at my feet,
> Nor what soft incense hangs upon the boughs,
> But, in embalmèd darkness, guess each sweet
> Wherewith the seasonable month endows
> The grass, the thicket, and the fruit-tree wild; 45
> White hawthorn, and the pastoral eglantine;
> Fast-fading violets cover'd up in leaves;
> And mid-May's eldest child,
> The coming musk-rose, full of dewy wine,
> The murmurous haunt of flies on summer eves. 50

In the starting part, the narrator blames himself for
the blindness of the thing itself, which can't help being
natural, since code either prevents humans from the
identification between them and it or is representative
of it. Namely, humans can recognise the thing itself, the
physical tree on a hill, through the medium of writing
or speaking. From the phenomenological view, readers
would feel it was difficult to understand—the tree itself
can never be meaningless—but when it enters into our
mind, it has this or that meaning through the thinking
process of it. This moment, the concept of the tree
in our mind can be called "noema" and the thinking
process "noesis." Thus, the tree in mind or code can't help
being alienated from the authentic shape and quality.

Additionally, the "absolute spirit" suggested by F. Hegel means the indirect process to the thing itself, since it emerges as a transformed shape by the intense trials of artists as a sculptor is carving some stone to represent a Pygmalion's beauty. As it is artists as a medium that can reveal this or that shape of the thing itself, so would God reveal itself through nature. Notwithstanding, the narrator yearns for direct experience with the thing itself instead of the recognition of its "guess" as connoted in the touchable, vivid things of "grass", "fruit", "tree", and "Hawthorn". The mission of the poet is suggested as "But, in embalmèd darkness, guess each sweet", as a blind man feels for the tricky road, only resorting to a delicate sense.

> Darkling I listen; and, for many a time
> I have been half in love with easeful Death,
> Call'd him soft names in many a musèd rhyme,
> To take into the air my quiet breath;
> Now more than ever seems it rich to die, 55
> To cease upon the midnight with no pain,
> While thou art pouring forth thy soul abroad
> In such an ecstasy!
> Still wouldst thou sing, and I have ears in vain—
> To thy high requiem become a sod. 60

Here the poetic narrator, as some scholars call the poet, strongly longs for Thanatos, as denoted in "To take into the air my quiet breath" with "requiem" played by the band of a nightingale. This reminds me of the magnificent requiem of A. Mozart rocking my mind in the movie *Amadeus*. But as Thanatos necessarily accompanies sensual pains, like aches generated on the moment of destruction of the body, s/he tries to avoid the tragedy by numbing our achy consciousness, our sense, or our body through "ecstasy" and "requiem" of the bird, beginning with the minor note. Namely, s/he yearns for the non-existential death in glee, armed with the transcendental spell of the esoteric bird, just like the patients of euthanasia intoxicated by sedative and Jesus ascending to heaven, guarded by transcendental divinity rather than the existential death in distress. But both the narrator and the bird fail to communicate with each other since cognitive humans and instinctual birds are incompatible in nature, as denoted in "Still wouldst thou sing, and I have ears in vain." Accordingly, he shall have died in thinking of the bird's twitter as the immortal "requiem", like an angel's trumpet. Compared with this grandiose situation, I recall the line of the Korean poem "Azalea", written by the famed Korean poet So-wol Kim: "When you are fed up with me/ and leave me,/ in spite of your death, I would never cry at all." Notwithstanding that the bird's song can't be confined to human letters, it may surely become a gospel.

Thou wast not born for death, immortal Bird!
No hungry generations tread thee down;
The voice I hear this passing night was heard
In ancient days by emperor and clown:
Perhaps the self-same song that found a path 65

Through the sad heart of Ruth, when, sick for
home,
She stood in tears amid the alien corn;
The same that ofttimes hath
Charm'd magic casements, opening on the foam
Of perilous seas, in faery lands forlorn. 70

The "Immortal Bird" exists in the poem "Sailing
to Byzantium" by Yeats: "To keep a drowsy Emperor
awake;/ Or set upon a golden bough to sing/ To lords
and ladies of Byzantium/ Of what is past, or passing,
or to come." The bird can overcross the historical,
physical space of past and present occupied by "emperor
and clown", belonging to the full and "hungry" classes.
Ruth's adherence to the realities of family life reflects
our regretful destiny, as we wish to stay in the memory
of the past. The memory erases our realities and forces
us to transcend them as seen in the novel *In Search of
Lost Time* (À la *recherche du temps perdu*, in French),
written by Marcel Proust. Sal Paradise, as a would-be
writer in the movie *On the Road*, directed by Walter
Salles, carried this novel with him wherever he went.
Humans have a tendency to head for a presence beyond
the creation of a foetus like Odyssey having tasted the
futile pleasures and returned to the home of maternity as
the space of Gaea. In this sense, we must leave each home
for the pursuit of whatever high or low goals we might
have so we feel nostalgic, like missing babies, though
now grown-ups, wherever we may go to find the toxic
material and symbolical sweets that contaminate our

intact body and soul beginning since the alienation from the womb, as connoted in "She stood in tears amid the alien corn," which would foretell the omen of Oedipus' wandering. The mysterious window opens to individual future, while "magic casements" would play a role of "siren", attracting curious humans looking out of each confined room willingly to make meaningful happenings out of otherwise meaningless lives.

> Forlorn! the very word is like a bell
> To toll me back from thee to my sole self!
> Adieu! the fancy cannot cheat so well
> As she is famed to do, deceiving elf.
> Adieu! adieu! thy plaintive anthem fades 75
> Past the near meadows, over the still stream,
> Up the hill-side; and now 'tis buried deep
> In the next valley-glades:
> Was it a vision, or a waking dream?
> Fled is that music:—do I wake or sleep?

Humans busily keep company with others and exchange friendships with each other for the justification or security of their existence. They flatter themselves by continually getting along with others. But personal appeal or affection to others is received and rebounded according to the counterparts' situations. Furthermore, the narrator's interest in the bird is unilateral in that s/he dogmatically interprets its situation in his/her shoes. Thus, although humans are solitary in nature, despite not being existentialists, they justify themselves as though they are not "Forlorn" and alone with surrounding things that seem to be united but separated. "Fancy," as a more organic thought than imagination suggested by S. T. Coleridge, would be a kind of anaesthetic that kills pains projected from sensual realities so that, when humans awake themselves, they come to feel pain again. The narrator complains of the changeable aspect of transient or whimsical "fancy" without immutability, as seen in "she is famed to do, deceiving elf." The bird's song spreads everywhere, as though the bell of a church delivers gospel in every direction. Also, according to a Buddhist view, it would be linked to the epiphany of *Avalokiteśvara* (a Buddha of compassion), but it never lessens the narrator's pain at all. What humans live in both consciousness and unconsciousness as seen in "do I wake or sleep?" can be paralleled with the famed Chinese philosopher Chuang-tzu's "dream of a butterfly" that he might be transformed into a butterfly in the dream. According to the principle of "intertextuality", a text is born from another text. As Chuang-tzu precedes Keats, may Keats parody his text?

In conclusion, The "Nightingale's" fantastic song as the thing itself that can temporarily numb the narrator fades out in the "glades" of the wood. Then the space of the song is replaced by some "forlorn" and desolate code, to which poets finally succumb, since they must express their feelings through code in the dimension of consciousness, as seen in "do I wake or sleep?", so that the extreme states of both "wake and sleep" compose our existences and realities, not needless of summoning

Dr Freud. Actually, humans can't clearly "wake" and "sleep" soundly at all, because the former situation would be disturbed by the shadow of a nightmare ("sleep"), while the latter would be haunted by the phantom of reality ("wake"). Notwithstanding, poets wrestle with the presence of the Nightingale's song as Ted Hughes, the British laureate poet, tried to hunt wild animals by fetters of letters. But the bird out of the magic "casement" endlessly tempts poets into entering the pits of self-delusion. It seems to be grasped like a three-dimensional reality but in vain, so humans and the bird individually run in opposite directions eternally.

This analysis focuses on "Ode on a Grecian Urn," which up till now has been known to be controversial and esoteric. Even though our views are naturally different, according to J. Derrida's "*differance*" (difference and deferment), the common opinions of the reading public or the community of interpretation given to this poem seem to be favourable or positive, even outstanding. Thus, we try to read this poem through the prism of colourful cultural concepts.

> Thou still unravish'd bride of quietness,
> Thou foster-child of silence and slow time,
> Sylvan historian, who canst thus express
> A flowery tale more sweetly than our rhyme:
> What leaf-fring'd legend haunts about thy shape
> Of deities or mortals, or of both,
> In Tempe or the dales of Arcady?
> What men or gods are these? What maidens loth?

What mad pursuit? What struggle to escape?
What pipes and timbrels? What wild ecstasy?

Readers, why does the "urn" become the "bride of quietness"? It is a taciturn thing in nature that never turns on its, but it can say to us only through some media, our mouths. Thus, it is alienated from humans in that the closer they want to get, the farther away from them it is. Rather, it is wrongly accused of the sin of temptation by cheating plaintiffs, humans, even though they would fabricate its identity. It has the original parents composed of soil and a potter, but it also has another parent, called time, that its living and dying destiny depends on as seen in "Thou foster-child of silence and slow time." The pot would be only a temporary, inauthentic object staying on the track of the running subject of "time" heading for the hazy, infinite myth. The constative, mythic narrative on the urn is intentional, artificial. Through its archaic pictures such as "men", "god", and "maiden", humans can reason that it would be complicated with some events. They are born from the pleasure of humans to kill time according to each taste and are made to be exchanged for food. The self-reference of the "urn" is reduced to an artist, like a reflection on the pond, unrelated to thing itself or truth. Namely, the tragic narrative on the Greek pot is linked to the real one of human history and is only a kind of the artificial plot of humans. The self-referencing of the pot is reduced to the poet's mind, not to the Greek mythic tale or the historical event. My idea can be diagrammed like this:

the pot → the poet → the poem as the creation of a new
myth
(a real thing) (medium) (a "simulacra" losing its reference)

> Heard melodies are sweet, but those unheard
> Are sweeter; therefore, ye soft pipes, play on;
> Not to the sensual ear, but, more endear'd,
> Pipe to the spirit ditties of no tone:
> Fair youth, beneath the trees, thou canst not leave
> Thy song, nor ever can those trees be bare;
> Bold Lover, never, never canst thou kiss,
> Though winning near the goal yet, do not grieve;
> She cannot fade, though thou hast not thy bliss,
> For ever wilt thou love, and she be fair!

The paradox of "heard" but "unheard" melodies
causes us to reason that even silence guaranteeing thing
itself as a communication of mind to mind by Buddha
can have a "sweeter" melody. But most humans must
feel bored of the taciturn melody like the tune of jazz
monotonously trembling in our ears. This would reflect
the narrator's mind more as yearning for a calm world
rather than a noisy one. We have two kinds of ears: sense
and "spirit" or "sensual" or spiritual. Above all, both
cases need the performance of a musician, whether the
melody can reach the audience's ears or minds according
to their dispositions. "Youth" should naturally enjoy his
energetic moment, needless of recalling the epicurean

maxim of "carpe diem" loyal to his dynamic entity, or will have repented of the vainly gone time.

Similarly, a poet or minstrel should write a poem or sing a song, as a nightingale always does for its own twittering entity like a garrulous wife's. Who is a "Bold Lover"? Is it either a Casanova or a Juliet? I think it is a poet as a chaser of the ultimate truth concerning life and death, but the moment he touches the truth, he must fade out of the realities because he is unleashed from the principle of gravity given to materials by destiny. Thus humans feeling gravity from the earth should climb up the unconquerable mountain of the truth, free from the earthly barriers such as gravity, pressure, weather, and human ecology, finally to go through its passages far shorter than the top until each death.

In this sense, though feeling the thirst for some spiritual or material aims day by day, humans can never be satisfied with anything else in the end, leaving much to be regretted. Thus, they can be divided into two kinds: physical and metaphysical people, or atheist and theist, according to each belief, philosophy, or disposition. Readers, which category do you want to belong to? The human mission on the earth is not to grasp the truth but to pursue it. If anyone would grasp the ultimate truth, even though the Absolute never allows us to do so, it is useless on the Earth, as it is not something secular, such as bread, wine, and gold, which are commonly beneficial.

Semiotically, it is because a horse on the chessboard is worthy of its existence among other horses while it lingers on it. In Christianity, God never allows humans to reach the truth but allows only Jesus, wearing the human mask of a carpenter, to save them. Even though humans feel the search for the truth is vain, what matters is that the burning desire for truth, origin, or root can never be extinguished easily. Namely, humans in nature have some eternal flames in mind to propel some "fair" goals irrelative to the final fruits, as revealed in "She cannot fade, though thou hast not thy bliss,/ For ever wilt thou love, and she be fair!"

> Ah, happy, happy boughs! that cannot shed
> Your leaves, nor ever bid the Spring adieu;
> And, happy melodist, unwearied,
> For ever piping songs for ever new;
> More happy love! more happy, happy love!
> For ever warm and still to be enjoy'd,
> For ever panting, and for ever young;
> All breathing human passion far above,
> That leaves a heart high-sorrowful and cloy'd,
> A burning forehead, and a parching tongue.

All things denoted in the stanza are the untouchable ones on the earth: evergreen "leaves" refusing a habitual farewell party with "spring", untired "melodist", "love" over love, undying "passion", eternal "young". Conversely, the narrator deplores the finite destiny of all the things on the earth that cause humans to feel "high-sorrowful and cloyed." This is why human life is filled with the succession of repeated actions: life and death, construction and destruction, things and arts, war and peace, return of seasons, meeting and parting, gain and loss, and mimesis and fact. Even in the desperate situations of humans, one can take comfort in the remark by R. S. Eliot, the American cardiologist: "Patients, you should enjoy them if your pains are unavoidable." Then what does "burning forehead" and "parching tongue" implicate? The former would mean the infinite wings of imagination or the capacity for abstraction, though in vain, given only to humans to comfort themselves as they are confined to the prison of the earth, while the latter would mean the rhetorical and deceitful discourses or opinions impatiently defined soon after feeling for the elephant of truth.

> Who are these coming to the sacrifice?
> To what green altar, O mysterious priest,
> Lead'st thou that heifer lowing at the skies,
> And all her silken flanks with garlands drest?
> What little town by river or sea shore,
> Or mountain-built with peaceful citadel,
> Is emptied of this folk, this pious morn?
> And, little town, thy streets for evermore
> Will silent be; and not a soul to tell
> Why thou art desolate, can e'er return.

For this continual myth in the pot's mural, the "priest" and his people sacrificed innocent "heifer" crying out at the sky on the bloody "altar" and then were cursed into ruin or dust. Likewise, this case would be similar to that of Jesus, son of God, accused of blasphemy by his countrymen, Jews and priests, and executed on the cross, and then the angry God dispelled the traitorous race, making them fall into the diaspora as the wanderers hanging about the world for nearly two thousand years. Or it seems that God cursed vicious people, dedicating innocent poets, like Keats, or good men, like the Samaritan, to the cause of greed beneficial to them, like the case of Sodom and Gomorrah, which left no trace. This penalty can be applied to an ecological view. These days, selfish humans have been sacrificing the innocent nature as their matrix to the scapegoat of civilization, whose "enlightenment project" has become a boomerang, returning to them at the risk of extinction.

> O Attic shape! Fair attitude! with brede
> Of marble men and maidens overwrought,
> With forest branches and the trodden weed;
> Thou, silent form, dost tease us out of thought
> As doth eternity: Cold Pastoral!
> When old age shall this generation waste,
> Thou shalt remain, in midst of other woe
> Than ours, a friend to man, to whom thou say'st,
> "Beauty is truth, truth beauty,—that is all
> Ye know on earth, and all ye need to know".

The last stanza reflects the narrator's despair at failing to verbally grasp the silent pot as the thing itself as connoted well in "Thou, silent form, dost tease us out of thought/ As doth eternity: Cold Pastoral!" At the same time, humans living in the flashy moment can never understand "eternity" excelling around the 4.6 billion-year history of the earth. The mission impossible of thinking animals, humans, is to admire the elegant Greek pot and its mural generation by generation. Thus it, though being a dusty being, says to them that it will outlive them with their passionate clapping, especially antique collectors. Namely, "truth" and "beauty" are the archaic pot itself, having "eternity" that humans should appreciate as suggested in "Beauty is truth, truth beauty,—that is all/ Ye know on earth, and all ye need to know". Unlike lions or tigers, humans as thinking animals can value the pot as an artefact becomes a barometer of the human condition. Or they are no better than animals if they lack secular vanity chasing the aura hovering around it.

In other words, this poem, as a cultural by-product, is both a truth and a beauty since it is the icon that all people have been trying to appreciate from the past to now. But why should we admire the cultural mass of mud irrelative to the human stomach feeling hunger, regarding it as something desirable? Would it be the kind of fetishism that the iconoclast, Andy Warhol, vehemently wanted to break?

CHAPTER 3

W. BLAKE: MARXISM OF HEAVEN

Called "the poet of vision" and admired by W. B. Yeats and T. S. Eliot, Blake raised the banner of the catch-phrase, "voluntary suspension of disbelief", though "semblance of truth", focusing on similarity is pre-conditioned, and headed for the world of vision or paradise in spite of being ridiculed by his contemporaries. However, I cannot confirm that he would ever reach an esoteric state, as Buddha would. Alternatively, I wonder if he was involved in occultism or cabalism. He agonized over the inevitable sufferings of life, especially on the human tragedy of the French Revolution, and he indulged himself in searching for the way of being unleashed from the hellish situations. Consequently, he produced the two themes: songs of innocence and experience, which seems to agree with M. Eliade's definition of the sacred and secular things of the world.

Additionally, this reminds me of I. Kant's concept: pure reason and practical reason. The former is concerned with time and space untainted by humans, while the latter is linked to physical participation in the pure elements as a boy plunges into the pond of time and space. In this sense, a song of innocence implicates any imaginary utopia beyond this world, while the experience of the song connotes the dystopia in the bloody realities of clothing, food, and shelter we resort to now. Can humans indulging in the "war of all against all" establish any paradise on earth? Blake tried to eradicate the three taboos suppressing humans: an unnatural orthodox religion, hierarchical political system producing the poor, and assumed common sense, structured by the five senses, or sense-data. In particular, he argued that some descriptions or comments seeming to be apparent or definitive couldn't enhance the imagination of the reading public; so he supported the poetics of ambiguity. Henceforth, we read four poems belonging to the songs of innocence and experience.

The first poem to read is "The Chimney-Sweeper", whose title blindly reminds us of Marxism and seems to hold the upper class as plunderers. But we can't deny that the world is composed of two extreme parts: high and low, plus and minus, male and female, bright and dark, and sky and earth. If the poor cleaner exists in London, the rich, not as the antagonists of communism, should exist in it to pay the fee. There is no way but for us to recognise this inconvenient truth. Thus, we should spread the intensity of humanity to the poor occupying the undeniable part of our community for its total well-being and security.

When my mother died I was very young,
And my father sold me while yet my tongue
Could scarcely cry "Weep! weep! weep! weep!"
So your chimneys I sweep, and in soot I sleep.

Why does this poem belong to the innocence songs? Is it because the orphan was pitiful and parentless? But we must recognise what is common. Even though he looked like a naive lamb, in reality he was contaminated quickly when born to be caught in the tough net of bloody survival, as seen in "So your chimneys I sweep, and in soot I sleep". Irrespective of the wealth or poverty of the family of birth, everybody is born into the abyss of sufferings: birth, ageing, illness, and death. Besides, the boy may be more pathetic, since he should go into "chimneys" every day for self-sufficiency. If the boy can't escape from the horrible environment, I think the only way to overcome it would be to enjoy it. Whatever location we may be born in, we shouldn't resent others and abuse ourselves but console ourselves, as we can't expect other to make a genuine effort on our behalf. Otherwise, we should suffer from a trauma of growth. In this sense, what Jesus born in the humble stable to predict his painful, sorrowful fate?

There's little Tom Dacre, who cried when his head,
That curled like a lamb's back, was shaved; so I said,
"Hush, Tom! never mind it, for, when your
head's bare,

You know that the soot cannot spoil your white
hair".

Why did Tom have his hair cut? Because the boy
should be fit for cleaning the chimneys. Namely, he should
become an appropriate tool to perform the job. Similarly,
we should adapt ourselves to the need of society, which
means castration of individual desire as the boy should
be castrated to become a castrato to entertain the Italian
nobility's ears as seen in the movie *Farinelli il Castrato*.
But what "white hair" should not be tainted by "soot"
would be squarely contrary to God's incomprehensible
Providence in that humans made of mud should be
determined to live in a world of mud including "soot",
sand, and dust, according to the Bible. Therefore, the
orphan's innocence can be incompatible with the human
stomach full of excrement unless s/he lives on dew and
cloud. This case would be similar to the logic that without
the penis there may be no sexual assault, which means
the denial of male existence. It is apparent that without
humans there are no sins and crimes.

And so he was quiet, and that very night,
As Tom was a-sleeping, he had such a sight!--
That thousands of sweepers, Dick, Joe, Ned, and
Jack,
Were all of them locked up in coffins of black.

And by came an angel, who had a bright key,
And he opened the coffins, and set them all free;

Then down a green plain, leaping, laughing,
they run
And wash in a river, and shine in the sun.

In his dream, an angel unleashed his friends
confined to each coffin, which would mean the hope
of an afterlife. Humans work for the contained space,
physical or spiritual, but want to transcend the stuffy
space though their feet are standing on the dirty world
of mud, notwithstanding that their heads are heading
for the paradise as the ambiguous existence of half-god
and half-animal.

Then naked and white, all their bags left behind,
They rise upon clouds, and sport in the wind;
And the angel told Tom, if he'd be a good boy,
He'd have God for his father, and never want joy.

Children led by an "angel" to weightless space and
liberated from much of the burden of life enjoy freedom
in their hearts. The omniscient narrator encourages us to
have a belief in God to secure the "joy" of paradise, just
like Pascal's wager. That's right. When humans look at
the mud, can they get a vision of a paradise in the sky?
They raise their sights and look up at the sky. Otherwise,
what they can see is only the earth as a grand dustbin
full of stinking trash.

And so Tom awoke, and we rose in the dark,
And got with our bags and our brushes to work.

Though the morning was cold, Tom was happy
and warm:
So, if all do their duty, they need not fear harm.

After "Tom" had seen the vision of paradise through
the angel's epiphany like the "Annunciation", he rather
strived to enjoy the tiring realities of chimney-sweepers
opposite to paradise. That might be a wise way. If we
suffer from an unavoidable pain, we had better enjoy it.
In conclusion, the narrator would stress the point that
humans captured by bitter pains on the earth can't help
exposing themselves to the limited situations so that
they can spiritually transcend the hell-like life through a
belief in God as revealed in "So, if all do their duty, they
need not fear harm".

When humans absurdly cast on the earth as some
existentialists complained resort to the planet, they
must feel frustrated to the extent of wishing for death
since they can never expect the afterlife. Alternatively,
they had better resort to any transcendental existence
than give up the belief of the "last leaf"—reminiscing
O. Henry, though abstract, hollow and invisible. Related
to this, if you follow Buddhism, you must endure the
physical pains of the grinding discipline, feeling a cramp
and paralysis with two legs crossed and mouth shut up
for some years until the raptured enlightenment. On the
other hand, if you choose Christianity, as Jesus died on
the cross for the sake of your original sins against God,
if you believe in Jesus as the Saviour, you are qualified
enough to go to Heaven. Thus, the thing you should do

is only to practice any choice to guarantee your afterlife. Or what other means? Without yearning for heaven, humans decline to the miserable parts of perishable materials composing the earth like pigs grunting in the sty, forgetting the sublime message of Michelangelo's "The Creation of Adam".

For the second poem, I am going to read "The Little Black Boy", including the theme of racial discrimination. So we feel the poet's comradeship toward humanitarianism in the risky homo-oriented society abhorring difference of colour. But his affection towards black humans would be seen as a generous sympathy of a master to his slaves.

> My mother bore me in the southern wild,
> And I am black, but O! my soul is white;
> White as an angel is the English child:
> But I am black as if bereav'd of light.

What "mother" functioning as Gaia "bore me" is a natural thing and I was born black innocently, unaware of the concept of skin colour. But humans arbitrarily have the biases between white and black and maltreat the black boy born from the providence of creation. Here the bitter, ferocious strife of hegemony happens to drive the two parts to the internecine wars such as the Civil War in America and Apartheid in the Republic of South Africa. To readjust the states of the prejudices, several black resistance intellectuals have come out onto the stage: Ngugi, Achebe, Fanon, and Martin

Luther King Jr. The narrator wisely indicates that the cause of becoming a black human would be the only thinner shining of the sun. Humans have no idea of the profound, sacred truth of diversity but tend to be immersed in the biased criticism of the strangeness or heterogeneity of the phenomenon. Namely, the fact that humans don't recognise the diversity of creation is to prove their blind position contained in the well of their superficial knowledge.

> My mother taught me underneath a tree
> And sitting down before the heat of day,
> She took me on her lap and kissed me,
> And pointing to the east began to say.

Although the stanza shows us the apparent description concerning the affectionate relationship between a mother and a son, this would not be all we can see. The black boy is tenderly sitting down with his mother in the shade screening the sun, which means the mise-en-scène of things. Things have a polyphonic nature rather than a monophonic one, so they have the two elements: bright and dark sides, such as sun and shade, which can be applied to the human case: white and black humans, so that we can enjoy the diversity of the world. Thus, black humans can never feel inferior to white humans, and white humans can never feel superior to black humans. The relation between the former and the latter is complementary. Accordingly, when a white human disregards a black human, it would be the self-denial of existence. What does "the east" connote? I wonder if it may indicate the diversity of directions such as rainbow colours.

> Look on the rising sun: there God does live
> And gives his light, and gives his heat away.
> And flowers and trees and beasts and men receive
> Comfort in morning joy in the noonday.

Here the merits of the "sun", presumably originated from God, are introduced to us: "light" and "heat" as the roles of a lamp and a boiler. If the "sun" wouldn't exist in the world, how can we live at all? Notwithstanding, we totally forget the blessing of photosynthesis as if we were the owner of the universe. The pouring, invaluable materials usually give us, if not being ascetics or monks, "comfort" and "joy". The "sun" never discriminates against the races based on colour.

> And we are put on earth a little space,
> That we may learn to bear the beams of love,
> And these black bodies and this sun-burnt face
> Is but a cloud, and like a shady grove.

Our lifespan is no more than one hundred years at most, out of a history of the earth that spans around 4.6 billion years. For the short term, we should try to learn the fire of love as the white would be white due to their ignorance of burning love. What does "to bear the beams of love" implicate? Black would be the sign or mark that love burns more. Thus, the blacks are more blessed and warm-hearted than the whites. Additionally, the blacks are concerned with unusual, curious beings brightened against the white earth such as "cloud" and "grove" as the special elements on the usual field and sky. On the other hand, this view may cause a reverse discrimination against the white.

> For when our souls have learn'd the heat to bear
> The cloud will vanish we shall hear his voice.
> Saying: come out from the grove my love & care,
> And round my golden tent like lambs rejoice.

The first line may afflict readers. What does "the heat to bear" implicate? I think we should understand that the white might receive the "heat" less, while the black might receive it more, which is all for humans to know since the thicker or thinner colours would not function as a major cause of mutual conflicts. This is the fact humans should know, whose recognition can become the motive for both sides to get along peacefully. Thus, "My golden tent" would connote the earthly paradise or the complete realisation of communism without any distinctions, though we can never expect that the miracle like the separation of the Red Sea in the Old Bible might come true realistically. The diverse colours of "lambs" only resulted from a difference of shade and would not matter before God. Thus, when some lambs attack or criticise other lambs, it would be a kind of self-abuse, ignoring the Providence of the Creator giving humans light and shade.

Thus did my mother say and kissed me,
And thus I say to little English boy.
When I from black and he from white cloud free,
And round the tent of God like lambs we joy:

This stanza focuses on the point of becoming beloved
"lambs" under the guidance of "God", irrespective of
the artificial preference of skin colours prior to nature.
Essentially, humans are disqualified from discussing this
or that creation as they are only pots made by the potter.
Of course, because the white boy has a selfish quality
as a descendant of Cain to enjoy priority over the black
boy, it may be difficult for both to get along in a friendly
manner in the eating-eaten jungle of the world.

I'll shade him from the heat till he can bear,
To lean in joy upon our father's knee.
And then I'll stand and stroke his silver hair,
And be like him and he will then love me.

In the last stanza, Jesus' humble stance to the strong is
exposed, which is that of reverse dedication and humanity
to the hostile, suppressive, white counterparts. Both of the
black cheeks should be trusted at the disposal of their hands
as Jesus did so over two thousand years ago. Paradoxically,
it means that only if the weak should understand the
strong, then true peace between the opposing powers
will manifest. Thus, the way the black boy would face the
white boy should not be struggle or hatred but humanity
and generosity. In this sense, "be like him" would mean

identification of nature based on altruism declining into neither any ideology nor local racialism.

The following poems concern the two poems belonging to the "songs of experience": "The Tyger" and "London". The former has been said to be a more abstruse and profound work than any other. But any interpretations up to now for this poem, immortal or amateurish, are open to readers with specific individual imagination and paralleled with the catch-phrase of "willing suspension of disbelief" of Romanticism.

> Tyger Tyger, burning bright,
> In the forests of the night;
> What immortal hand or eye,
> Could frame thy fearful symmetry?

The first stanza shows us the surprising description of a horrible tiger. When we think of the tiger, we would regard the animal as a sacred being, further a patron saint. Also, tiger, though extinct in the Korean peninsula since several decade years ago, still functions as a symbolic animal of the Korean totemism with bear. Anyway, "tyger" might be admired as a "sublime" existence beyond description. Why did the First Cause create this uncanny predator? That is the unsolvable search for the existence. We, humans, have the sole mission to appreciate the beauty of the "symmetry" pattern without knowing the background of its creation as we are phenomenal existences only playing on the crust of the earth.

In what distant deeps or skies
Burnt the fire of thine eyes?
On what wings dare he aspire?
What the hand, dare seize the fire?

This stanza shows us the untouchable charisma of the predator. The stately beast reigns over the unlimited area as seen "In what distant deeps or skies". Its fiery eyes illuminate the dark world and agile limbs like "wings" may jump up to the top of the sky and the avaricious claws may grasp even fire. On the other hand, this would suggest to us the ideal of a hero able to save this troubled, painful world such as the valorous and sagacious leader with the quality of a lion and fox argued by N. Machiavelli.

And what shoulder, & what art,
Could twist the sinews of thy heart?
And when thy heart began to beat,
What dread hand? & what dread feet?

This stanza shows us the awe of the almighty maker of the beast like the muscular Achilles. Simultaneously, it connotes the dynamism of the energetic beast of the whole empowered and combined by part and part such as "heart", "hand" and "feet". The super engine is wrapped in the sumptuous leather. Who made the "tyger" like the fishes existing in the pond at a deep mountain? What purpose? Of course, these questions belong to agnosticism, though numerous scholars across the world are striving to explore

the essence of a thing itself till now so that they have found
quantum as the least unit of a thing itself.

> What the hammer? what the chain,
> In what furnace was thy brain?
> What the anvil? what dread grasp,
> Dare its deadly terrors clasp!

In the human dimension, the tools to make artefacts
are suggested such as "hammer", "furnace", and "anvil",
which reminds us of the scenery of a blacksmith's shop in
a countryside. Humans try to reproduce a tiger, but what
they make, at best, is no more than a mechanical, coarse,
dead model compared with the biological, delicate, live
one. Of course, for the case of biological cloning, what
humans can do is only to choose genes like male-female
dating not to raise the complex of genes and to inspire
it with a spirit. By what artificial means can humans
generate the esoteric "deadly terrors" that the tiger
emits? But in the light of God, these tools are useless
since God utilises earth/water/ fire/wind and inspires
them with life force whenever God makes things.

> When the stars threw down their spears
> And water'd heaven with their tears:
> Did he smile his work to see?
> Did he who made the Lamb make thee?

The narrator would be complaining about the
contradictory world since wildness and sacredness

co-exist as tigers and rabbits live in the same mountain. A tsunami sweeps a hopeful newlywed couple lying down on the beach and deer are chased by lions as seen in "Did he who made the Lamb make thee?" In this sense, humans are confined to the Coliseum, where friends and enemies struggle to outlive each other to the end, which would be God's masterpiece. The narrator asks us who knows the paradoxical providence of Genesis. In addition, the description of the darting "stars" and crying "heaven" and God's "smile" is reduced to a contrived self-reference. Thus, our belief in God should be blind because we can never understand God's creation, contrary to logic programmed as an *a priori* condition in the human mind.

> Tyger Tyger burning bright,
> In the forests of the night:
> What immortal hand or eye,
> Dare frame thy fearful symmetry?

This poem reminds me of the horrible painting "Scream", by Edvard Munch, which points to the world of dystopia. That is because the world is composed of the two hostile elements: lion and deer, male and female, good and evil, success and failure, friend and foe, and light and darkness, which would mean the opposition of "fearful symmetry" or the rigid homogeneity or balance of the right and left sides of the tiger's face.

The following poem is "London", the centre of capitalism as the source of the "Industrial Revolution".

This is the moment all materials began to hide behind exchange value or nominal value. Those competent in handling figure or logic could possess more property than those incompetent in doing so. Roughly speaking, the poem accuses the city of inhumanity and brutality. Let's read the poem in detail by way of either close reading that modernists favour or "misreading" that postmodernists favour.

> I wander thro' each charter'd street,
> Near where the charter'd Thames does flow.
> And mark in every face I meet
> Marks of weakness, marks of woe.
> In every cry of every Man,
> In every Infants cry of fear,
> In every voice: in every ban,
> The mind-forg'd manacles I hear

The dystopian realities in London are unfolded frankly. Of course, the hell-like situations must equally happen in all the metropolises in the world including Seoul, New York, Paris, and Tokyo. That could be converged on the catastrophe of natural selection or daily human affairs without God. According to Genesis, humans should live exhausting lives suffering from other humans, the competition of community and nemesis of nature and even themselves as seen from the symptoms of narcissism, self-delusion, and self-abuse. In London, humans should do something good or should not do anything bad to conform to common interest rather than personal interest according to social convention seen in "each charter'd street".

> How the Chimney-sweepers cry
> Every blackning Church appalls,
> And the hapless Soldiers sigh
> Runs in blood down Palace walls

Here, several kinds of pains are apparently exposed to readers, who may think of the stanza as having no room to be decoded further. But we can find the basic model of Marxism. According to the structure of community argued by Marxists, "base" and "superstructure" are rendered such as "sweepers", "soldiers", "Church", and "Palace". The church depends on "sweepers" but is directly unhelpful, though spiritually helpful, to them. Soldiers dedicate themselves to the "palace", but the latter would take their burdensome, annoying services for granted. How would the noble queen think of her "soldiers" bogged down in the mire? How could the "church" feed the hungry "sweepers", as Jesus practised feeding several thousand people with five loaves of bread and two fishes?

> But most thro' midnight streets I hear
> How the youthful Harlots curse
> Blasts the new-born Infants tear
> And blights with plagues the Marriage hearse

Through the tragic scenery happening at a "midnight" of London, readers may shudder, feeling identified with the narrator. This unpleasant mood leads us to Nietzsche's chilly, desperate vision of the world. By the way, he ironically regarded the tragic life as the natural life in his masterpiece, *The Birth of Tragedy*, while the Greek had viewed human life as tragic life so that they might have tried to forget the miserable life caused by their birth through dreamlike arts searching for Apollo giving humans the enlightenment and pleasure of knowledge.

Realistically, Nietzsche saw that humans could never avoid destruction or death so that he had better indulge himself in the Dionysian ways that create things through destruction as a pre-condition of construction.

Namely, I think, the Greek might have tasted a paradoxical bliss of life from the tragedy favoured by Aristotle, which would be an idea of masochism. Thus, this stanza would connote a forced, ironic pleasure of life such as "curse", "tear", and "marriage" that caused through the unavoidable tragic scenery of perishable life like the tear-shedding but laughing life as seen in the last scene of the movie *The 25th Hour* starring Anthony Quinn, in which he, returning home after being discharged from the army, forcedly smiled with "cheese" to take an amicable picture of his family plus his extramarital child born between his wife and a Russian soldier in the midst of the Second World War.

CHAPTER 4

S. T. COLERIDGE: DYNAMICS OF IMAGINATION

Romanticism reminds us of "Strum und Drang" (storm and stress) in German, and Coleridge in England would be the poet fittest for the fanatic trend. Another term pops up before us, "willing suspension of disbelief", which suggests that however a poem may derail from convention, we would be better to heartily appreciate the fantasy rather than doubting it. This term is also useful in post-humanism that reality is changed into "hyper-reality" suggested by J. Baudrillard. The former would have its reference or origin as a boy on the way home, but the latter would have no reference or origin as a self-referential or self-reflectional thing or a lost child. Extrinsically, he used opium to activate his mind to the maximum, or I wonder if he would take opium to console himself fatigued from his realities.

He divided state of mind into two parts: imagination and fancy. The former can be divided into the two types: primary and secondary. The primary one would be concerned with the perception of these or those impressions derived from outer things grasped through our senses, which everybody can perceive. But the secondary one, belonging to esoteric, poetic vision, would deviate from the universal perceptions sensed by the primary one and result in some artistic, fantastic recreation or representation so that it can unite and modify several ordinary things into some novel things. I wonder if the "secondary imagination" as a magical power would be linked to "interdisciplinary convergence" of heterogeneous fields. It combines inner forces such as will, emotion, reason, perception, intellect and passion, and converges something internal/external and subjective/objective on some creative aim or point. The secondary one would be similar to chameleonic functions of dream suggested by Dr. Freud: "displacement", "distortion", "condensation", and "secondary elaboration".

For imagination, we reminisce on C. G. Jung focusing on human symbolic realities in that humans are composed of an inner part like archetypes or primordial images and an outer part like persona or symbol. Imagination would function as a necessary means linking symbols to archetypes and archetypes would be self-realised through symbols such as "anima", "animus", "shadow", etc. He used "active imagination" to bridge the gap between dreams and realities. Unlike this, Lacan as a structuralist saw humans trapped in the net of language and regarded imagination as a childish mechanism tied to and freely hovering over the symbol. For Christianity, imagination can be the useful, hopeful medium of faith to confirm Heaven. Also, M. McLuhan, a forerunner of medium, would naturally view imagination as expansion of conscious as if robot is that of body. With the advent of the era of J. Baudrillard, Coleridge's archaic imagination will ironically burst into re-bloom. Now, we can think of "fancy" as argued by Coleridge. The term can never fly unleashed from the conscious, but it is no other than memory with fixity free from time and space like imagination.

Now, we are reading his famed poem, "Frost at Midnight", whose title reminds us of some bitter realities. What causes the phenomenon on the earth to trigger as the Big Bang did? Whose plot or intention? But even humans called wise Homo sapiens have had no idea of it but have hopelessly been suffering the good or bad influences.

> The frost performs its secret ministry,
> Unhelped by any wind. The owlet's cry
> Came loud—and hark, again! loud as before.

In the atmosphere of the closed system, the sacred mission given to chilling "frost" at night, free from the sunlight, is to freeze the land loosed by day in which humans are imprisoned and never unleashed without an exodus from this planet. Thus, they are like colourful birds such as "owlet" and "hark" confined to the magnificent cage. Of course, the chirps sound louder on a silent night than on a noisy day. By the way, though easily overlooked, what may the relation between "frost" and two kinds of bird implicate? I think the sound of the two

birds would run parallel with groundless human noise or
forced freewill not affecting the circulation of nature at
all, but the silence of frost would be concerned with the
immanent will of nature circulating and rearranging the
environments of the earth.

> The inmates of my cottage, all at rest,
> Have left me to that solitude, which suits
> Abstruser musings: save that at my side
> My cradled infant slumbers peacefully.

Here, we, though hard, find a view of structuralism,
which means dichotomy embedded in the text. This is a
revolutionary trial to find a novel meaning rather than
the stereotyped interpretation like the rest, peace, and
speculation caused by nocturnal silence as seen in "My
cradled infant slumbers peacefully". That is composed of
the oppositional pairs: night and day, silence and noise,
"slumbers" and conscious, "solitude" and participation,
"inmates" and strangers, "frost" and thaw, and "musings"
and action. Hence, what composes the world depends
on the oppositional dichotomy of things visible and
invisible. The static "musings" can become a potential
part of human action and the silent "slumbers" can
become a dormant way of human life.

> 'Tis calm indeed! so calm, that it disturbs
> And vexes meditation with its strange
> And extreme silentness. Sea, hill, and wood,
> This populous village! Sea, and hill, and wood,

With all the numberless goings-on of life,
Inaudible as dreams! the thin blue flame
Lies on my low-burnt fire, and quivers not;
Only that film, which fluttered on the grate,
Still flutters there, the sole unquiet thing.

In the silence of the deep mountain temple, monks
with their feet crossed focus on each specific theme for
enlightenment called as Koan: "Pull the bird out of the
bottle!" and "Why did the high monk, Dharma, come
from the east?" By the way, the narrator says that "silence"
would rather bother meditation. Thus, readers know that
silence and meditation belong to the same category, but
are now confused into a state of anomie. We can think of
the same cases, though not exact. Rest rather interrupts
rest and some books are the barriers to understanding
other books. Something identical disturbs the same kind
as monks become other monks' foes as in the Buddhist
maxim that when monks encounter other monks, they
should kill them. For something to expose itself, it should
be different from other things. Human life is composed
of "goings-on", like accidents, and their surroundings,
such as "sea", "hill", and "wood". And energy or life force
like "fire" is needed for biological existence so that its
emittance and "unquiet" extinction as "blue flame" must
be accompanied.

Methinks, its motion in this hush of nature
Gives it dim sympathies with me who live,

Making it a companionable form,
Whose puny flaps and freaks the idling Spirit
By its own moods interprets, everywhere
Echo or mirror seeking of itself,
And makes a toy of Thought

For affluence and maturity of life, there would be contradictorily needed not only "silence", peace, and "musings", but also noises and "goings-on too". But it is only humans that can feel curious about some meanings of things and sense spiritual pains. Fiery passion instigates the "idling Spirit" as a hesitative forerunner as if it could make a revolution, which resorts to "its own moods" only to fall into "a toy of Thought" implicating "maya" as a Buddhist idea.

But O! how oft,
How oft, at school, with most believing mind,
Presageful, have I gazed upon the bars,
To watch that fluttering stranger! and as oft
With unclosed lids, already had I dreamt
Of my sweet birthplace, and the old church-tower,
Whose bells, the poor man's only music, rang
From morn to evening, all the hot Fair-day,
So sweetly, that they stirred and haunted me
With a wild pleasure, falling on mine ear
Most like articulate sounds of things to come!
So gazed I, till the soothing things I dreamt
Lulled me to sleep, and sleep prolonged my dreams!

When the narrator looks at the fire and meditates on it, do you remember the French scientific philosopher Gaston Bachelard's "Poetics of Reverie"? The narrator would gaze at the dying fireplace in the frosty, cold night, moving visible to invisible dimension. This would be concerned with the "mechanism of defence", as referred to the "grate" to guarding people against the bitter cold, the church "bells" to comfort the poor, and the "dreams" to fill all dissatisfied people with something supplementary, metaphoric for a homeostasis of life. Here, both the secular and sacred sounds based on home and "church" would be all the same to people living in a purgatory of the earth, since both are something selfish and indifferent to God. This would reflect the narrator's pessimistic mind arising from the frosty, chilly night, but he looks up to Heaven for a breakthrough in life.

> And so I brooded all the following morn,
> Awed by the stern preceptor's face, mine eye
> Fixed with mock study on my swimming book:
> Save if the door half opened, and I snatched
> A hasty glance, and still my heart leaped up,
> For still I hoped to see the stranger's face,
> Townsman, or aunt, or sister more beloved,
> My playmate when we both were clothed alike!

That humans exist in should pre-condition the conscious level rather than the unconscious one so that we can verify our existences. Namely, our hazy reveries should cease and move to the aching realities as our dreams should be retrieved in the realities. According to Dr Freud, this can be linked to the two principles of reality and pleasure. Teachers' falcon-eyes haunt and censor even children's dreams so that the latter would be tamed by the former to result in the birth of subjects fit for the community. Indulged in "mock study" as a practice of mimesis following its convention such as rules and norms, subjects with the same impersonality as cars from the Ford motor should continually dedicate themselves to the honourable tradition of the community, or they should perish.

> Dear babe, that sleepest cradled by my side,
> Whose gentle breathings, heard in this deep calm,
> Fill up the interspersed vacancies
> And momentary pauses of the thought!
> My babe so beautiful! it thrills my heart
> With tender gladness, thus to look at thee,
> And think that thou shalt learn far other lore
> And in far other scenes! For I was reared
> In the great city, pent 'mid cloisters dim,
> And saw nought lovely but the sky and stars.

Existential "breathings" emitted from "babe" reign over vain "thought" so that the ontological dimension would precede the epistemological one. And babe's immense potentialities excel the narrator's stuffy realities that an adult must face. "Cloisters" favouring symbols like the monastery seen in the movie *The Name of the Rose*, based on the book by Umberto Eco, would function as a mechanism of oppression to castrate the narrator's desire in that he "saw nought lovely but the sky and stars".

> But thou, my babe! shalt wander like a breeze
> By lakes and sandy shores, beneath the crags
> Of ancient mountain, and beneath the clouds,
> Which image in their bulk both lakes and shores
> And mountain crags: so shalt thou see and hear
> The lovely shapes and sounds intelligible
> Of that eternal language, which thy God
> Utters, who fro eternity doth teach
> Himself in all, and all things in himself.
> Great universal Teacher! he shall mould
> They spirit, and by giving make it ask.

Why does "babe" emerge in the frost at a night? He would symbolise Jesus to save the then double-risky world as connoted in "Frost in Midnight". It is why any adults immersed or dyed in the sophisticated knowledge of the world can't save the world. They are being bogged down in the internecine mire of environments they voluntarily arrange as we are trapped in the net we cast. Thus, the narrator would rather yearn for the *a priori* state than enter into the plot of the "symbolic order" camouflaging the essence of things with a dehydrated code. Absurdly, God demands that God "moulds" the human "spirit" and urged it to save the world God created though God is omnipotent. As seen in the Bible, only a "babe" free from

the clichéd commonsense of the world can encounter
God as the "Great universal Teacher". Hence it is natural
that babe can exist because God as the Cause of the Big
Bang exists.

> Therefore all seasons shall be sweet to thee,
> Whether the summer clothe the general earth
> With greenness, or the redbreast sit and sing
> Betwixt the tufts of snow on the bare branch
> Of mossy apple-tree, while the nigh thatch
> Smokes in the sunthaw; whether the eve-drops fall
> Heard only in the trances of the blast,
> Or if the secret ministry of frost
> Shall hang them up in silent icicles,
> Quietly shining to the quiet Moon.

The last part reminds us of some indifferent state
and of the phenomena of nature—windy, rainy, stormy,
or frosty—as seen in "all seasons shall be sweet to thee",
but if we were innocent like a "babe," we would have
no fear of the horrible elements as "babe" has no idea
of them. How can "babe" know the horror of tsunami
indeed? Though collective unconscious should not be
disregarded, a babe would have no fear of even a tiger.
Consequently, humans stand in the given environments,
nature, whose cause they never know and are structuring
some cultures as the structured environments as naive
children are building a sand castle at the beach in which
the mountainous, ferocious tides seem to dash toward
them, never knowing why "eve-drops" are changed into

"icicles" and what the purpose of "frost" is. Namely, "babe" would be closer to the truth or presence of "frost" that blinds grown-ups wrapped in the code or symbol of "frost" so that the former would be identified with nature or "frost", while the latter would be alienated from it. Innocent "babe" can put her fingers into the mouth of a dog, while intelligent adults can never do it. Likewise, this poem reveals the enigmatic epiphany of "frost" as a truth to us simply rather than implicating the double risks of winter, cold, and fear.

Next, let's read "Melancholy. A Fragment". Some critics or academic advisers would criticise us for getting astray in the maze of the text or going wide off the mark. It doesn't matter, since no one can hit the ghost-like target but indulges into self-reference, deeper or more shallow.

> Stretched on a mouldered Abbey's broadest wall,
> Where ruining ivies propped the ruins steep--
> Her folded arms wrapping her tattered pall,
> Had Melancholy mused herself to sleep.

This part reminds us of Baudelaire's "Le Spleen de Paris" (The Blue Paris) in that vitality is completely disregarded and rather cursed as the motive of destruction as a dying baby reproaches her parents. What "mouldered" wall decorated with "ivies" means can be thought of as the contrast between authentic and inauthentic things. But prior to discussing the priority of either side, of course, though the plant would be preferred, both of them will have shared the inevitable fate of disappearance. In this sense, in the narrator's nihilistic sight, everything would head for a decline with a quick or slow pace, which must make readers blue. The "steep" but crumbling wall and vivid but dry ivies would have no distance, which causes the narrator to feel "melancholy" as a vacancy of existence.

> The fern was pressed beneath her hair,
> The dark green adder's tongue was there;
> And still as past the flagging sea-gale weak,
> The long lank leaf bowed fluttering o'er her cheek.

The *mise-en-scène* of things is unfolded like a panorama of a ghetto. Those are replaced such as the grassroots suffering from the glorious ivies of the upper class, danger disguised as a superficial peace, weather repeating good or bad result, and something feeble resorting to something brazen.

> That pallid cheek was flushed: her eager look
> Beamed eloquent in slumber! Inly wrought,
> Imperfect sounds her moving lips forsook,
> And her bent forehead worked with troubled thought.
> Strange was the dream-----

Chasing truth results in the "pallid cheek" like pale scholars in the labs blocked off the sun, robbed of blood, and alerts us not to speak of it prematurely, as revealed in "Imperfect sounds her moving lips forsook". The plant, ivies, would be symbolised as "eager" scholars or poets dreaming a "strange" dream, unlike an ordinary one, searching for the truth of things, as seen in the *Indiana Jones* series. Accordingly, the rigid "wall", like the Great Wall in China, may stand for human chronicle history, "ivies" for temporary, desiring human life and "melancholy" for the human mechanism of defence and alerting us to the tough realities of surviving others as "ivies" grow encroaching the "wall". On the other hand, the narrator would point to the then inflated dilettantism ignorant of the essence of nature in that the "ivies" are covering over the "wall" of longstanding historicity, endlessly spanning since the Big Bang and vainly growing dried. What does "Strange was the dream" connote? May it be the ferocious, horrible, internecine vision to slaughter several hundred thousand people by a single nuclear bomb with which A. B. Nobel thankfully presented them and to destruct the skyscrapers by the aeroplanes? Of course, the barbaric human deeds committed by the descendants of Cain, who killed his brother, would never be "strange" but natural. Of course, there would be the other keener analyses in our open horizon of English poetry.

CHAPTER 5

W. B. YEATS: TEXT OF BLISS

I. Prelude: Blind man touching an elephant

As inspired by "He. Opinion is not worth a rush" in "Michael Robartes and the Dancer", inviting a dialectic discussion until now, with the advent of the queer era of even favouring "misreading" in the post-modern generation, dogmatic, and obstinate arguments on texts are overshadowed by the theory of "the death of author" refuting creation and authorship and further justifying plagiarism. Now, the authoritative interpretations on the literary canon fade away from our sight. This trend can be recognized as a postmodern or deconstructive one, but I contend that it does not need to be rationalized as one of the recent trends in the antique tradition of English literature since the birth of *Beowulf*, in that since every human has each vision for things from birth, it is natural that s/he looks at them differently.

Accordingly, for platonic critics or authors to coerce readers into one standardised interpretation on a canon is an autocratic idea. For the ultimate matter between reading and "misreading", argued by Harold Bloom on texts conjuring up this moment, I think that it doesn't matter, since none naturally can reach the *idea* or presence of things, including canon, human, desk, and tree. Simultaneously, I wouldn't like to welcome ways of "horizon of expectations" practiced by "reception theory" and indulged into a subjective position alienated from community as is the *modus vivendi* of American transcendentalists; for human is fatefully confined to a code system and influenced by the discourse of others which triggers the retrieval of "library theory" by Jorge Luis Borges as an unconscious langue lurking behind a job. Therefore, interpretations on texts may be foregrounded according to each reader's level of literacy, based on each cultural background, and would be dependent on each intellectual quality, composed of inborn talent and acquired craft, which forces us to reminisce on Michael Riffaterre's argument stressing literary competence. So constitutional views on texts can't be recognised as something desirable.

From this perspective, I try to escape from the established interpretations on Yeats' poems and avoid the monotonously generalised comments of the poems, but I can't help confessing the impossibility of the perfect escape as realised in the movie *The Shawshank Redemption* and ending up with a practice of arbitrary or unfamiliar imitation. This stance would be concerned with the two views that R. Barthes risks pursuing when looking at a photo in *Camera Lucida*, "stadium" and "punctum". For my henceforth provocative position on Yeats' text, the latter in pursuit of the connotative meaning of things is preferred to the former recognising the denotative one. In this respect, the bright audience at this conference to comprehend my paper seems to be collinear with those reacting diversely to the models provided by Rorschach ink-blot test or the semiotics or Gestalt psychology.

The theme of the following esoteric poem "Michael Robartes and the Dancer" as the mysterious piece of Blake's greatest disciple applicable to Jungian approach (Raine 5) has been said to reveal the unity of being in that the former functions as a male persona and the latter as a half-self or a kind of his anima. Of course, according to J. Lacan's assertion, I can't escape from the experience of individuation reigned over by the unconscious discourse of others or langue, but I strive to resist the stereotyped reservoir of mind and enjoy a sort of language game only as a *Homo Ludens*. For expecting an interpretative cooperation from the famed voluminous canon, *Yeats* (Oxford: Oxford UP, 1970) by Harold Bloom, with the parched heart craving for a drop of rain, I searched and searched for the authoritative comment on "Michael Robartes and the Dancer", but in vain except the sarcastic grumbles in the three poems "Demon and Beast", "The Second Coming" and "A Prayer for my Daughter" included in the same collection (Bloom 313–27). Retrospectively, this would be a habitual gesture having occurred still, relying on the referential interpretations of some reputed critics for a sacred literary text and rationalising the symptom as the postmodern ideology of "intertextuality". Against my will favouring and referring to precedent interpretations on the poem, inevitably I play a role of the initiator on the arbitrary interpretation of the poem. But this awkward interpretation should be renewed by the destructive or natural principle of "difference" and "deferment", argued by J. Derrida continually.

II. Pleasure of a Creative Imitation

He. Opinion is not worth a rush;
In this altar-piece the knight,
Who grips his long spear so to push
That dragon through the fading light,
Loved the lady; and it's plain 5
The half-dead dragon was her thought,
That every morning rose again
And dug its claws and shrieked and fought.
Could the impossible come to pass
She would have time to turn her eyes, 10
Her lover thought, upon the glass
And on the instant would grow wise.

Here I don't refer to any references for exploring the identity of "Michael Robartes" for fear of being influenced by its established ideas, leading to falling down into the generalisation of interpretation. But this could be, somehow, a conscious trial disregarding unconscious level remaining invisible but visible. Inevitably, I can't help being affected by a "discourse of others" because of being born in a code system so that Harold Bloom's maxim "anxiety of influence" can be sustained. For analysing this poem, I don't consider thinking of apprehending the identity of Mr. "Robartes" reminding me of "J. Alfred Prufrock" as a model of the modern man normalised into the modern Western society. Superficially speaking, he is believed to be a man possible to be interpellated as Mr. Mandarin.

As Indiana Jones went through the crust of the earth in pursuit of the Holy Grail, I should look at the denotative aspect of the poem. The main signifiers are "Knight", "dragon", and "lady" as the medium for us to be able to infer a typical romance, which would be the generalisation of myth that R. Barthes hated. The "knight" functions as a Samaritan in that he saved the miserable girl groaning in a trap of the devil. Instead of that, I intend to look at this poetic situation as a political one, which appears tinted with an indication of post-colonialism. In this sense, "Knight" can be replaced by a hero or saviour that can face against the tyranny of "dragon" as an oppressor and "lady" as a "subaltern" kindling the memory of Antonio Gramsci and Julia Kristeva. The prediction following or supporting these signifiers implicates the action and reaction of bitter struggles.

She. You mean they argued.

He. Put it so;

But bear in mind your lover's wage 15
Is what your looking-glass can show,
And that he will turn green with rage
At all that is not pictured there.

She. May I not put myself to college?

He. Go pluck Athena by the hair; 20
For what mere book can grant a knowledge
With an impassioned gravity
Appropriate to that beating breast,
That vigorous thigh, that dreaming eye?
And may the devil take the rest. 25

Pondering how to read this part, I can see how the human personality is formed in the system of a normal community. Correspondingly, "The Mirror stage", activated by J. Lacan, shows us that what ego would be built through the mirror like the other's sight may be nothing but misrecognition, so for us to know something truly is no more than ignorance. In the respect, there are three views to surveil humans. First is the view of Olympus for the Creator to overlook them. Second are the views of others, including governors and supervisors, to help result in the birth of autonomy in custody through heteronomy for M. Foucault to patent worldwide. Third is the narcissistic view for everyone to look at his/her own image on the water or mirror. In spite of these diverse views, it is something impossible for humans to know themselves, so what they know is no more than some fragmental contents or a crust of reality. Further, what humans would be afterwards is confined to the appearance of the Thing-Itself, incompatible with the authentic passage of searching for the Holy Grail as the Ultimate Truth. Thus, what humans can do on the earth is merely to produce fabulous meanings of Things with the help of libidinal power, Eros. Even reaching this digital era that human intelligence has grown best since the Renaissance, I don't care whether humans are crouched inside or outside the dark cave regretfully contrary to F. Bacon's theory of icons. Accordingly, wherever they may exist in, the state of their blindness remains the same. In other words, humans are experiencing only the duration of the denotative extension of materials, transformations of materials, as humans are finally reduced to the soil, whose reason is unknown and hidden as the apocalyptic conspiracy refusing to reveal itself.

The "wage" for "knight" truly to demand as the reward of his sacrifices is for "she" to reflect on her history having lived in helplessness and thoughtlessness through the "mirror". This can be concerned with the servile adaptation of colonial dominations, as a grim proof of dehumanisation, called "black skin – white mask" coined by F. Fanon. It causes "he" to have "rage" if "she" should not practice the earnest advice of "he" and his help becomes in vain. The moment I read these lines I retrieved the juvenile canon, *The Jungle Book* (1894) by Rudyard Kipling, ostensibly decorated with the pure and touching friendship between a boy Mowgli and wild animals, however, currently to be degraded to a text of colonialism to justify the domination of India, according to post-colonial whims.

On the other hand, Kipling can be innocent in that humans can't help being influenced by the ideology of an imperial or inferior community they belong to, in that arts are the productions that reflect community as their matrix, comparable with the inseparable relation between water and fish, which can refer to "reflection theory" by György Lukács as a forerunner of socialist realism, and in that citizen's consciousness is fatefully reduced to the indigenous discourse of nation as his Other. This could be recognised as a model of "political unconsciousness" suggested by F. Jameson, but it is difficult to be exempt from the suspicion of *dolus eventualis*(willful negligence). Back to the lines 19–25, the thing to be absolutely necessary for "she" is not the platonic and easygoing education of "collage" but daring and unbending struggles against "dragon", like an empire, operating soul and body signified in "beating breast", "vigorous thigh", and "dreaming eye" of vision. In other words, what the male poetic persona desires may not indicate Mahatma Gandhi's peace parade but Malcolm X's radical activism. Hesitating the resistance movement would be equal to the follies of the "devil" who God damns.

> She. And must no beautiful woman be
> Learned like a man?
>
> He. Paul Veronese
> And all his sacred company

Imagined bodies all their days 30
By the lagoon you love so much,
For proud, soft, ceremonious proof
That all must come to sight and touch;
While Michael Angelo's Sistine roof
His "Morning" and his "Night" disclose 35
How sinew that has been pulled tight,
Or it may be loosened in repose,
Can rule by supernatural right
Yet be but sinew.

Unlike the cowardly hesitation of Hamlet's style, metaphor daringly functions and demonstrates its performance to transform things into monsters. It is a principle of our life to change and imitate something. In the sense "Paul Veronese" can be seen to stand for woman's valour and boldness in that his painting style in the Renaissance expressed a woman's body boldly. Thus, I can see that Ireland, symbolized as a miserable woman in shyness and frustration by sovereign powers, as I say previously, should unveil herself before the world rather than being couched and self-contained in the blurry world of myth and legend recollecting "Aengus" in "Innisfree", which can consult "Imagined bodies all their days/ By the lagoon". Additionally, what a woman should do to save the country is to awake herself from illiteracy and helplessness into rationalism and positivism sensible in "For proud, soft, ceremonious proof/ That all must come to sight and touch". In short, for the grand revolution of Ireland, physical and mental strength should be needed. Even though the poetic narrator usually put Christianity less, what means in "Michelangelo's Sistine roof" represents "Genesis" by the Creator. But it is my claim that its significance may connote transforming into the independence and revolution of Ireland from her voluntary enervation and involuntary subordination to remake the new epoch of homeland by her own will and "sinew" alerting to "repose" in the lines 37–9.

She. I have heard said 40
There is great danger in the body.

He. Did God in portioning wine and bread
Give man His thought or His mere body?

She. My wretched dragon is perplexed.

He. I have principles to prove me right. 45
It follows from this Latin text
That blest souls are not composite,
And that all beautiful women may
Live in uncomposite blessedness,
And lead us to the like - if they 50
Will banish every thought, unless
The lineaments that please their view
When the long looking-glass is full,
Even from the foot-sole think it too.

She. They say such different things at school. 55

To resist the negative elements spread inside and outside Ireland, the mind and body should be disciplined to dispel the concern felt in "There is great danger in the body". But our body originally hates the pain of realities, for the cosiness of the embryonic period would be automatically inscribed in the body, since humans are comfortably couched in the agreeable womb. Then, as humans naturally face the defiance of troublesome and wearisome realities that the body housing a soul grows worse with age finally to lose each soul, they lack the harmony of totality uniting "thought" and "body", which brings about the catastrophes of the individual, community, and country as good as the case of a headless Frankenstein. I see that "wretched dragon" may mean a dominator or colonialist withered as a result of the awakening of the Irish. "He" himself functions as a messenger of truth as revealed in line 45: "I have principles to prove me right" recorded in solemn "Latin" as normative alphabets which can let us remember the Kantian proposition: "Act only according to that maxim by which you can at the same time will that it should become a universal law."

"He" is emphatic on "blest souls" wrapped in integrity above the chaos of odds and ends that the Irish should inevitably undergo for the rehabilitation of Ireland. I would like to see this purity as a crescendo of pure patriotism. In this sense, "all beautiful women" may stand for the Irish and should be armed with "uncomposite" and unsophisticated virtue. It can be inferred that "He" as one of the national leaders who "lead us to the like" has the same destiny as King Arthur would wish for while leading the Celts to Avalon. Desirable results demand desirable conditions as a practice of causation felt in lines 50–4: "if they/ Will banish every thought, unless/ The lineaments that please their view/ When the long looking-glass is full,/ Even from the foot-sole think it too". The first condition may be to discard idle thought and the second one may deserve a glorious body confirmed in an inner mirror as the noble descendants of King Arthur so dutifully as to sacrifice themselves for the homeland, not seeking individual interest and greed. But "She" seemed to have a wavering conviction of patriotism for Ireland despite his earlier passionate eloquence as sensed in the last line: "They say such different things at school." I think it may suggest a kind of disagreement or chaos of national affairs.

III. Conclusion: Possible to read of truth/text/life?

Humans never touch the Ultimate Truth like the origin of things or source of material or transcendental signifieds, namely the source of self-sufficient meaning. What they can do at best is to pose specific positions by relative subjectivism that allows numerous subjects to express each imaginable view on things. If humans reached something absolute, it would be meaningless for them to stay alive on the earth. It is why merely as humans hold five senses, they can feel and recognise

Things realistically or romantically before crossing to Hades. This could be synonymous with the case of a moth rushing into the fire after flying around a lamplight as a bodhi tree of nirvana. As soon as it plunges itself into the fire and then is in communion with fire, it becomes a senseless or meaningless object like particles of dust, transferring the sensible into the insensible dimension. Accordingly, humans share the same destiny with moths in that both pursue the Ultimate Truth or the sacred fire respectively even though their entities are different originally as being intelligible or instinctual. In this sense, we never know the reverse side of things but we now justify our positions composed of individual guesswork or imagination or doxa, hovering around the lamp of truth and yearning for the vain state of nirvana. Frankly speaking, our various ideas may end up with an anthology of "simulacrum" franchised by J. Baudrillard.

Besides, for Buddhism, when a human transcends himself into the state of homeostasis like nirvana of stillness, meaning extinction of desire, this world full of greasy and burning desires surely would be meaningless for Buddha arguing for overcoming our fatal and material dimension (birth, ageing, illness, and death) without clinical proofs, halting the wheel of *samsara*. Comparably, Moses longed for meeting God; instead, he received the slate in which God's commandments were engraved, since if he had met God as the Sun of Truth, he would have burnt out like the moth. Thus, it would be extremely fortunate for the sake of humans that God appeared in the medium of fire and voice in the Bible, reminding us of the "Da" of "What the Thunder Said" in *The Waste Land*. Simultaneously, we can retrieve the myth of King Midas to make anything he touched gold and to give up the magic power to become one of the common. What can the superman who can make all things gold and is exempted from the lack of material things envy in the world? Hence, the moment humans are united with divinity getting out of the material, the meanings of all things comprised of material in the world naturally would be discarded.

The Truth humans are desperately chasing now is really a relative thing that each individual produces according to each view, causing "contrast-effect" and a poetic thing possessed in a maya of words. Similarly, it may be very unwise for Dr. Faust to gain occult power to reign over the world and deal in his soul to the devil. If the doctor reaches the state of self-sufficiency, he would lose his existence as a material being cornered in an incomplete state changeable with age. In short, a human, to maintain her existence while living with memorizing the "tragic joy" or whatever, had better hold an incomplete state desiring completeness, so it is natural that he should behave just like a greedy human haunted by the ghost of drive, giving up the empty ambition immune from pitiless principles of nature ruling over time and space, which is why a supposed super-human, who transcends the limit of the human and takes off the mask of the human as a Buddha achieving absolute freedom or removal of the persona, finally goes back to the profane and corrupt human market. In the sacred situation, becoming a living god like Colonel Kurtz in *Apocalypse Now* (1979). What for?

Concerned with this point, it can be assumed that the theory of cave icons has some fallacy in that the human originally has self-insufficiency irrespective of wherever the human may live inside or outside the cave, further regardless of the rhetoric of the glimmering light illuminating junks in the cave. What a human knows of something is to recognize its part, not its whole, which likewise signifies that what a human knows of a human through the knowledge of "transcendental subject" derided by post-modernists, even though contrary to "now-here" subject "dasein" checking Icarus' epistemological navigation, is truly to be ignorant of the human.

In this poem, which implicates "political unconsciousness" to urge the Irish to struggle against inner and outer enemies, the dialogue between "he" and "she" denotes the essential condition necessary for the process of individuation as "growing pain" applied to both individual and country, Ireland, and proves a dialectical relation of human existence that human identity can't be slanted toward one side, male or female. This can be connected with M. Bakhtin's "dialogism" focusing on the simultaneous presence of diverse existences based on "polyphony". Equally, my radical interpretation to Yeats' poem shouldn't be constructed solely and should be replaced incessantly according to the principle of "difference and deferment" in view of the reciprocal delimitation between me and others that can never escape from the world of the panopticon.

Works Cited

Bloom, Harold. *Yeats*. New York: Yale UP, 1972.

Culler, Jonathan. *Literary Theory: A Very Short Introduction*. Oxford: Oxford UP, 1997.

Friedman, Barton R. *Adventures in the Deeps of the Mind*. Princeton: Princeton UP, 1977.

Howes, Marjorie. *Yeats's Nations: Gender, Class, and Irishness*. Cambridge: Cambridge UP, 1996.

Raine, Kathleen. *From Blake to A Vision*. Dublin: The Dolmen Press, 1979.

Ramratnam, Malati. *W. B. Yeats and The Craft of Verse*. Lanham: UP of America, 1985.

Schricker, Gale C. *A New Species of Man: The Poetic Persona of W. B. Yeats*. Lewisburg: Bucknell UP, 1982.

Timm, Eitel. *W. B. Yeats: A Century of Criticism*. Columbia: Camden House, 1990.

Yeats, W. B. *The Collected Poems of W. B. Yeats*. ed. Richard J. Finneran. Scribner Paperback Poetry: New York, 1996.

CHAPTER 6

R. FROST: TRUTH IN UNIVERSAL THINGS

The poet generally reminds me, a citizen of the third world, of the poem "The Road not Taken", ensuring his international recognition, in which the narrator yearns for the other way of life. But humans should not be allowed to scan and then choose every way like Zeus flying over Mount Olympus, which makes humans feel limited, local, temporary existences. Especially, unlike other poets, noble and platonic, he dedicated himself into the tough realities as a factory hand and a farmer. Hence it would be a careless, hotheaded misconception that his poems could be easy for readers to understand. Though he processed natural elements and represented pastoral environments, they would implicate some esoteric epiphany concerning an essence of life. Namely, his ontological approach to things makes readers feel some sacred meanings behind universal things.

One of the works standing for the poet, "Stopping by Woods on a Snowy Evening" is known as the orientation of Thanatos. But this generalisation should be renovated, withstanding the orthodox resistance of modernism on the basis of the prism of reading horizon since close reading means a misreading. Readers should declare the independence of reading unleashed from the despotic authority of famed overseas critics according to the platform of postmodernism resisting the absolute truth of things. Now let's read this poem and spread each wing of imagination though my intervention remains awkward.

> Whose woods these are I think I know.
> His house is in the village though;
> He will not see me stopping here
> To watch his woods fill up with snow.

As readers usually regard this poem as a simple work, this stanza looks simple, but, I think, it has some complicated floating meanings. For "woods" to exist in the world, they should reside in my mind that can grasp their existence as the concept that "I know". There happens the keen opposition between the knowledge of wood and the existence of wood. This sparks the phenomenal or *a priori* view since, to know wood, it should reside in my mind. But even before I recollect "his house", it apparently pre-exists as seen in J. Lacan's maxim: "I think where I am not, therefore I am where I do not think". Of course, "I" can be replaced by "he". He has no idea that I am thinking of his house. This moment "I" would become an existential other or a non-existential other. Since he can't see "I" watching his "woods" now, this would be concerned with the situation of "panopticon" suggested by M. Foucault. Thus "I" and "he" and the others compose the world, keeping mutually alienated states and not knowing the individual situation.

> My little horse must think it queer
> To stop without a farmhouse near
> Between the woods and frozen lake
> The darkest evening of the year.

Here, the distance between "horse" and "I" can be confirmed, confined to the chains of instinct and reason. The former pursues biological need, while the latter overlooks it. The elements such as "woods", "frozen lake", and "darkest evening" threaten the narrator, and readers can sense the risks enough. Hence the narrator should survive the terrible elements to restore peace of mind, which implicates natural selection. Also, the narrator should have some power to hold the reins of the horse.

> He gives his harness bells a shake
> To ask if there is some mistake.
> The only other sound's the sweep
> Of easy wind and downy flake.

The kinds of "sound" suggested in the stanza are separated into the two parts: artificial and natural. The former has semiotic meanings for communication, while the latter groans through "wind". This moment humans should communicate with the horse and "wind". The two elements function as a kind of siren alerting "I" to dangers: mistake and coldness. Thus, the three elements stand in each position. In the meantime, "Bells" can function as a sign or medium to link between "I" and the horse faced with the bitter environments arranged by the winter. The human parallels the horse and the seasonal shapes at individual will.

> The woods are lovely, dark and deep,
> But I have promises to keep,
> And miles to go before I sleep,
> And miles to go before I sleep.

The narrator exposes self-oriented trends to us as in "The woods are lovely, dark and deep". The presence, like "woods" without feelings, is the absolute thing that "I" should love rather than expecting its love. Regardless of nature's will, "I" have a will to practice "promises" to destruct nature for self-realisation like a painter or a designer to grasp a perspective of nature. Through this poem, we can perceive human life decorated with solitude and indifference since "I" am alienated from "he" as the wood owner, horse and natural elements. Namely, the promises I should keep have nothing to do with nature's will. The narrator musing the *mise-en-scène* of things would undergo a kind of crisis of existence in the critical situation surrounded by the rival environments, like existentialists searching for a cause of existence. As a whole, this poem is not a general lyric or bucolic one, singing the beauty of nature and the following catharsis, but a participatory one, containing the fierce consciousness of survival, so it would expose a sanguinary reality to readers.

Now, readers can taste his masterpiece, "After Apple-Picking", whose interpretations are controversial still. The only animals considering the situation "after apple-picking" are humans as half animals since other animals are usually indifferent to the situation of after-meal. This would focus on a moral action for humans to differ from other animals only loyal to instinct.

> My long two-pointed ladders sticking through
> a tree
> Toward heaven still,
> And there's a barrel that I didn't fill
> Beside it, and there may be two or three
> Apples I didn't pick upon some bough.
> But I am done with apple-picking now.
> Essence of winter sleep is on the night,
> The scent of apples: I am drowsing off.

Time and space as "pure reason" of the foundation of experience spread out before readers. Here the narrator's action as "practical reason" suggested by I. Kant is added. The "picking" happens at an "apple" orchard in the "winter". What does the "ladder" and insufficient "barrel" mean? I think the former would represent our insatiable desire like Prometheus' or Icarus', and the latter would connote our unfinished desire. However, the narrator sticks to the temperate stance as seen in "two or three/ Apples I didn't pick upon some bough". In addition, the nature-oriented mind is exposed to us as seen in "winter sleep" and felt satisfied with "scent of apples" rather than a gold bar.

> I cannot rub the strangeness from my sight
> I got from looking through a pane of glass
> I skimmed this morning from the drinking trough
> And held against the world of hoary grass.
> It melted, and I let it fall and break.

Here, a phenomenal recognition is revealed since the narrator can grasp things or apples through the medium of sight gathering sense data such as "glass", "trough", and "grass". Thus, the narrator would agree to the phenomenal or Kantian idea, suggesting noema/noesis and the likelihood of the phenomenon. Namely, what humans can see would be no more than recognition of a thing or an apple rather than a bare thing or an apple itself. Furthermore, although the poet didn't major in phenomenology, he would show readers some phenomenal thought through this part. The narrator would resist the principle of nature to mobilise winter and freeze things as seen in "It melted, and I let it fall and break", in which "It melt" would mean a natural point and "I let it fall and break" an artificial one. The "strangeness" would mean an ultimate doubt as to why all things should be intimidated and frozen in winter.

But I was well
Upon my way to sleep before it fell,
And I could tell
What form my dreaming was about to take.
Magnified apples appear and disappear,
Stem end and blossom end,
And every fleck of russet showing clear.

Here, I think, "before it fell" would mean before it was dark or before the night visited so that it can be linked to "dreaming". The magical dream-work suggested by the narrator is compatible with Dr Freud's theory that dream would be no less than a reflection or oppression of reality as seen in "Magnified apples appear and disappear,/ Stem end and blossom end,/ And every fleck of russet showing clear".

My instep arch not only keeps the ache,
It keeps the pressure of a ladder-round.
I feel the ladder sway as the boughs bend.
And I keep hearing from the cellar bin
The rumbling sound
Of load on load of apples coming in.

Nature wants humans that harvest it to experience the same pain as it does. That emerges as some causational symptom like the "ache" of "My instep arch" as revealed in "I feel the ladder sway as the boughs bend". Notwithstanding, the narrator is ever intoxicated by

"The scent of apples" piled in the warehouse and stays in the euphoria arranged by self-justification that labour causes happiness of fatigue. And what the narrator can hear as the sound of the apples would be an illusion resulting from the amplification of the imagination.

> For I have had too much
> Of apple-picking: I am overtired
> Of the great harvest I myself desired.
> There were ten thousand thousand fruit to touch,
> Cherish in hand, lift down, and not let fall.

Humans are always exhausted due to their desire descending to the unseen bottom as seen in "I am overtired/ Of the great harvest I myself desired". They have an overflowing greed pursuing much more amount of apples than they need, so the extra amount is exchanged into a nominal value like currency, giving others the chances to taste the apples. Unlike other animals, humans don't desire to be full in each stomach now, but the satiety should last to the future through currency as the nominal value of apples.

> For all
> That struck the earth,
> No matter if not bruised or spiked with stubble,
> Went surely to the cider-apple heap
> As of no worth.

Naturally, this or that formed apples fallen on the earth according to the principle of gravity can be categorised into the standards that humans have set: for either goods to sell or juice, though nature has never divided all things into either this or that kind. Similarly, humans have divided skins into either white or colours so that they strengthen the colonial dogma that the former is prior to the latter, disregarding the rainbow's diversity.

> One can see what will trouble
> This sleep of mine, whatever sleep it is.
> Were he not gone,
> The woodchuck could say whether it's like his
> Long sleep, as I describe its coming on,
> Or just some human sleep.

Here the two views of "sleep" are suggested: humans and "woodchuck". But the former can sleep an uneasy sleep since they are the sole thinking subjects out of all things. Conscious daily affairs are flowing into unconsciousness transformed into the imagery of a dream. Thus, when they seem to sleep deeply, they can't actually sleep well since the transformed imagery of the conscious daily routine or unfulfilled desire would afflict them. As suggested by J. Lacan, human thinking in which they physically never exist would be a nightmare derived from the ferocious realities removing the apples from the matrix. As humans hurriedly repeat the cycle of labour and rest, the wild rats would be somewhat fearful and hunted since they are besieged with more powerful carnivorous enemies such as wild cats and wolves. The narrator would think of her sleep as a nightmare haunted by the imagery of daily faults like robbing fruit of trees so that her life could become uncomfortable all day and night.

Thus he would envy the unselfish life of the mere "woodchuck" because the animal would be happy only if it can be stuffed. I think that may be wrong. The rat would be unhappy because it is surrounded by more powerful animals in the food chain so that it should be chased and nervous anywhere it hides. Though death as an eternal sleep would ensure eternal peace, in Buddhist view, sleep could never be comfortable since humans would be caught in the trap of "samsara" as the causation that the actions of this world demand, and also in Christianity the horrible last judgment of heaven would be waiting for humans as fatal, determined sinners.

CHAPTER 7

T. S. ELIOT: EXISTENTIAL STRIFE

Since attending college, I have been much charmed in Eliot's poems and up to now have interpreted a few poems of Eliot's in a few of the academic journals concerned with English literature in Korea— "The Love Song of J. Alfred Prufrock", "The Waste Land", and "Ash-Wednesday"—while still not attempting to interpret "Four Quartets" as his swan song. Not only his famed poems but also his criticisms on literature and culture should never be overlooked. There are the theory of "objective correlative" caused from his oriental doubt of the tongue or language accessing a thing itself and "platinum theory" saying of poet's functions as a medium or catalyst between humans and things, and "theory of impersonality" that poets would be affected by the dead artists or poets and the theory of "tradition and individual talent" that individuals should continually dedicate themselves to tradition and become a part of the gigantic chronological monument or archive.

Henceforth, let's read "Whispers of Immortality" and "Hysteria". Though readers may regard the poems as minor ones, I think the poems are worthy of being much appreciated.

> Webster was much possessed by death
> And saw the skull beneath the skin;
> And breastless creatures under ground
> Leaned backward with a lipless grin.

I saw a medical student put a skeleton on his messy desk, lovingly patting it like a pet. Once the skull might have been this or that person with blood and flesh having a burning passion and greedy ambition, but with age, he was weathered to the bone. I understand enough when King Solomon in the Old Bible might have thought of his life like a drop of dew mistily disappearing in the morning, "Webster" as his descendant cries out, "vain, vain and vain". Similarly, this stanza provides a helpless transience of life for readers. Like this, the young, muscular, powerful body capable of beating even a monster shall have become more lifeless and more exhausted against gravity and pressure finally to the last shelter of the metal coffin. Even though human youth shall struggle with the weathered elements and head for the obscure underground, readers should enjoy this moment with reading the desperate but witty lines of human beings and only making a "grin", not expecting any other means.

> Daffodil bulbs instead of balls 5
> Stared from the sockets of the eyes!

He knew that thought clings round dead limbs
Tightening its lusts and luxuries.

This stanza shows us the same dismal, blue tone
as seen in Thomas Gray's "Elegy Written in a Country
Churchyard" or Charles Baudelaire's "The Flowers of
Evil". The example of natural assimilation is suggested.
A human body absent-minded as material in origin
was naturalised in the underground, and the "daffodil
bulbs" of the elegant flowers replaced the (eye-) "balls"
and absorbed the nourishment from the rotten corpse
as dignified, brilliant lotus flowers as the symbol of
Buddhism feed on the filthy mire. This connotes the
treacherous contradiction of life: the daffodil and the
corpse, the lotus and the mire, and the sacred thing
and the secular thing. The narrator grieves for the
termination of a futile life and regards lofty "thought",
burning "lusts", and precious "luxuries" as inauthentic
wastes. What is apparent is that the very affairs
happening after death are not concerned with human
capacity at all: body to prey of bacteria and soul to hell
or heaven. Thus, what humans should do is only to feel,
appreciate and represent things on the earth.

Donne, I suppose, was such another
Who found no substitute for sense; 10
To seize and clutch and penetrate,
Expert beyond experience

What is the "substitute for sense"? That is the literal scream as a code shouting out when aching. But that is not enough to represent the cellular "sense". The terrible sense data of being speared hides itself behind its utterance or signifier. I understand the narrator's complaint, since Donne might not have lived in a full-fledged literal, symbolic culture like today's era full of code. Notwithstanding, the accesses to a sense of both past and present would not be different from each other surprisingly because they should arbitrarily use the medium of sense. Sense would be the experience that we should feel rather than speaking of it. Who is the "Expert beyond experience"? I think that may be a super-man not undergoing human discipline or a monk with enlightenment.

> He knew the anguish of the marrow
> The ague of the skeleton;
> No contact possible to flesh 15
> Allayed the fever of the bone.
> ....

The narrator is searching for some transcendental experiences that the hermit Donne tried and failed to accomplish. The real pains of the "marrow" and "skeleton" as ingredients of the body can't be solved by superficial entertainment or treatment such as massaging, caressing, and taking medicine. Those would be concerned with the origin and purpose of the body, which never stays within human knowledge. If so, what does "fever of the bone" connote? I think it would mean the nostalgia of its origin that the stimulation of "flesh" never affects as if the disabled without limbs must be obsessed by them.

> Grishkin is nice: her Russian eye
> Is underlined for emphasis;
> Uncorseted, her friendly bust
> Gives promise of pneumatic bliss. 20

This stanza shows us her captivating figure as a gorgeous prostitute, "Grishkin", seducing men. But as this cognition would be too stale, we must inquire into another fresher one. An idea hit me, which is temporality of life in that the juicy beauty will shortly stay with the girl as a skin-deep phenomenon.

> The couched Brazilian jaguar
> Compels the scampering marmoset
> With subtle effluence of cat;
> Grishkin has a maisonette;

Why does "Jaguar" drive out "marmoset"? I don't know the truth well, but I have a rational idea or guesswork of the happening. It may be an instinctual measure for survival, as an attack method to guard himself in the open wild, what the animal can solely do is only to use her body organs such as teeth, claws, roaring, and "effluence" rather than a knife or a gun or a cannon. But to protect themselves from other antagonistic humans, they should conceal themselves

in an artificial shelter such as a physical "maisonette"
and a metaphysical convention or treaty. In conclusion,
this stanza would reveal that animals rely on authentic
things, while humans depend on inauthentic things.

> The sleek Brazilian jaguar 25
> Does not in its arboreal gloom
> Distil so rank a feline smell
> As Grishkin in a drawing-room.

This stanza would be concerned with human
redundancy or surplus value. Unlike this, I can recognise
that it would easily remind readers of female estrus
that "jaguar" and "Grishkin" connote. As the human
imagination, the painkiller given us by the Creator to
transcend our troublesome realities, is optional for us to
use, we can't offer the criticism that any interpretations
to this stanza would be blind or awkward. The cat emits
her smell linked to the mating season, but the woman
would never succumb to the rule, which means the
surplus of sexuality regardless of the mating season.
The former doesn't practice more desire than necessary,
compared with the latter wielding more desire than
necessary and never satisfied with even the surplus
food mountainously stored in the warehouse. In this
sense, ironically the cat would be similar to a temperate
monk not allowing redundancy, while humans would
be like avaricious animals. The common point of the
two creations is brutally waiting for an unfortunate

prey, lurking in different residences such as an "arboreal gloom" and "drawing-room".

> And even the Abstract Entities
> Circumambulate her charm; 30
> But our lot [scholars] crawls between dry ribs
> To keep our metaphysics warm.

For this stanza, I think, the acute contrast between material and metaphysics is revealed as connoted in "And even the Abstract Entities/ Circumambulate her charm". Regretfully, what humans have completed since genesis still is only numerous self-referential or narcissistic principles, laws, and theories of nature and God: inauthentic artefacts irrelevant to the essence of nature. Namely, semiologically, the signifiers and signifieds on trees themselves frantically dance. By the way, reaching the last part of "But our lot scholars crawls between dry ribs/ To keep our metaphysics warm", readers may feel dizzy. I think, though famed feminists in the world must be irritated, as revealed in "But our lot scholars crawls between dry ribs/ To keep our metaphysics warm", "our lot" like male scholars should yearn for a fleshy "Grishkin" as the result of male "ribs" created by God to complement confusing, vain metaphysics such as poetics or philosophy or other academies. The "dry ribs" would connote a kind of skin-deep beauty, though unevenly.

The next poem for us to read is "Hysteria", which indicates dissatisfaction. As Dr Freud proclaimed, the psychological symptom is said to expose itself, motivated by the female's vacant womb. Conversely, I wonder if this poem might have been produced by the poet's lack of maternity caused by his neurotic wife.

> As she laughed I was aware of becoming involved in her laughter and being part of it, until her teeth were only accidental stars with a talent for squad-drill.

When "she laughed" with opening her mouth, "I" surrendered to "her." Readers, what do you think of it? I think that they would be involved in love affairs. By the way, the next line afflicts me, so I am wandering to chase my logic for the lines for a while. What does it connote? An idea hit me—that when she flaps her lips with white "teeth", symbolizing a shiny bullet to penetrate the male's heart, which would mean "squad-drill" as a light operation by the duo, our sexuality for reproduction is interrupted and we fail to reach orgasm, which would result in a lack of desire, causing "hysteria".

Therefore, I think, "stars" connotes not constellations, as everybody can easily read them, but would connote useful means compatible with white "teeth". Of course, there may be other critics who do not agree with my interpretation. Namely, when a male and a female make instinctual love, her burst of speech would castrate our sexuality. Our physical love used to end by an "accidental", symbolic quarrel. This moment we can reminisce the episode that dates back to the Greek era, the erotic relation between Socrates and his wicked wife, Xantippe, broke due to her nagging. Additionally, the unfortunate relation between T. S. Eliot and his nervous wife, Vivienne, followed the previous case.

> I was drawn in by short gasps, inhaled at each momentary recovery, lost finally in the dark caverns of her throat, bruised by the ripple of unseen muscles.

This situation would be concerned with the natural convergence of male and female from a biological view. Or this would show us the dedication of others in that the duo should be the necessary existences complementarily composing each life: males exist for females and vice versa.

> An elderly waiter with trembling hands was hurriedly spreading a piece of pink and white checked cloth over the rusty green iron table, saying:

What sacred mission would an "elderly waiter" have? He plays the role of a medium or agent for the young duo to lead to the symbolic order or the horizon of a community. As an inauthentic existence, he habitually practices phallic ceremony to succeed human symbolic tradition: law, rule, manners, convention, treaty and contract to buffer human relations. In the Lacanian view, he executes the "Name of the Father" for the continuity of community as revealed in "spreading a pink and white checked cloth over the rusty green iron table". Namely, though inauthentic, the traditional, sterile elderly help the authentic young to practice reproduction for the sustainment of the community like a hotel "waiter".

> "If the lady and gentleman wish to take their tea in the garden, if the lady and gentleman wish to take their tea in the garden …"

This part may perplex or confuse readers. What do the same double subordinate clauses connote? I reason, this would mean the human identity: repetitive modes of life. A writer is writing a novel to reach a Tolstoy's level, a pitcher wishing for a Nolan Ryan in the major league is continually throwing balls at the strike zone, and an actor dreaming of becoming a Dustin Hoffman in Hollywood is rehearsing actions fit for a movie. But all humans can't reach their aims and can't help staying in lack of desire so that they would suffer from "hysteria".

> I decided that if the shaking of her breasts could be stopped, some of the fragments of the afternoon might be collected, and I concentrated my attention with careful subtlety towards this end.

There would be the cultural enlightenment such as manners and custom that the old would give to the young for the continual succession of human institutions. That would mean that only if they can be unleashed from instinctual dimension they can build a human-like culture based on reason and rationality. Thus, their desire would be castrated, and they would eternally yearn for the lack transforming into "hysteria" as revealed in "I concentrated my attention with careful subtlety to this end". Briefly, the realistic concentration on each aim of life would drive a nostalgia for the origin of life. Additionally, the old have urged the young to adapt themselves to ISA (ideological state apparatuses) as the host of ideology, suggested by the French sociologist Louis Althusser, such as government, court, school, police, army, hospital and diplomatic agents, and to succeed the sticky tradition of survival on the earth, when the young are born into some social subjects wearing the masks of "interpellation" such as Tom's dad, professor, Mr President, sergeant, etc. In conclusion, for humans, they can't completely demonstrate their desire but can partially do it, so its remainder would be entered into the unconscious, implicating the magma of dissatisfied "hysteria".

CHAPTER 8

WALLACE STEVENS: NIETZSCHEAN PHANTOM

As readers know, Stevens majored in law and enjoyed diverse careers: reporter, lawyer, writer, and businessman in an insurance firm. Like F. Kafka and T. S. Eliot, his job was in the finance field, though money and literature would appear to be incompatible. He made his poetry debut at the age of 35, perhaps too late to become a poet, as it is said that a would-be poet should be in his teens. His poetic trends would be romantic, symbolic, and impressionistic. In his lifetime, his name was unknown, as was the case with several remarkable artists, but he got the posthumous fame as an immortal poet in Western society.

His themes would be mainly focused on the "transformations of imagination", which means that he was sure to be influenced by G. Santayana regarding reality as a delusion of presence, as well as Paul Klee and P. Cezanne, who also doubted the fixed views of things. In his view, imagination is not a kind of consciousness, and reality is not the same concept as the world since it remains outside our mind. Reality is the fruit of our imagination's doing, not static but dynamic in the poet's mind. In his thought, the poem functions as the medium of missing God. There would be some severe tension between the shapes the world gives us and our imagination flying away from them. But our overflowing and wayward imagination should be contained into the rigid vessel of concepts castrated and produced by the reason as the best one out of human devices to recognise the world. Standing on this perplexed crossroads between imagination and reality, Stevens lingered painfully, doubting the entity of presence caused by the world.

Readers, let's read the poem, "Sunday Morning", as his magnum opus that made him posthumously famous across the world. Rather than skipping over the poem here and there as most scholars have done, we are going to go through the lines of each stanza irrelative to understanding it well like a bull rushing across the wild field.

I

Complacencies of the peignoir, and late
Coffee and oranges in a sunny chair,
And the green freedom of a cockatoo
Upon a rug mingle to dissipate
The holy hush of ancient sacrifice.
She dreams a little, and she feels the dark
Encroachment of that old catastrophe,
As a calm darkens among water-lights.

The pungent oranges and bright, green wings
Seem things in some procession of the dead,
Winding across wide water, without sound.
The day is like wide water, without sound,
Stilled for the passing of her dreaming feet
Over the seas, to silent Palestine,
Dominion of the blood and sepulchre.

The first stanza shows us the two principles suggested
by Dr Freud: "reality and pleasure" principles, since free
"Sunday" is the day concerned with rigid and ascetic
Christianity. The former urges us to come to the muddy
realities of the human market, but the latter stirs us to
be at our will just like an unleashed colt disregarding
social censorship. In "the dark Encroachment of that
old catastrophe", we can reason the cause of the human
tragedy, which results from Eve's fault in Genesis, and
which would be linked to Jesus' rebirth and the formation
of Christianity reigning over human minds. But what
does "As a calm darkens among water-lights" connote?
It would mean that weighty silence gets the colour of
"water" to be thicker and thicker psychically. Namely, the
darkness and silence surrounding her can function as the
matrix of her gloomy destiny. Juicy "orange" and brisk
"wing" are reduced to "procession of the dead". That's
right. Something alive in some days becomes something
"dead", whose cursed fate can be consoled by Sunday,
"the day" of recreation and the day of Jesus' rebirth.
"The day is like wide water" taking and leading painful
humans to paradise or Moses' miracle of the Red Sea in

the Old Testament. Namely, "Sunday" would be the day of salvation that can save all humans only if they believe in the Owner of Eden as the subject of the Big Bang.

II

Why should she give her bounty to the dead?
What is divinity if it can come
Only in silent shadows and in dreams?
Shall she not find in comforts of the sun,
In pungent fruit and bright, green wings, or else
In any balm or beauty of the earth,
Things to be cherished like the thought of heaven?
Divinity must live within herself:
Passions of rain, or moods in falling snow;
Grievings in loneliness, or unsubdued
Elations when the forest blooms; gusty
Emotions on wet roads on autumn nights;
All pleasures and all pains, remembering
The bough of summer and the winter branch.
These are the measures destined for her soul.

Here who is "she" rather than he? I think "she" would be metaphoric of the humans as would-be brides waiting for the "second coming" of Jesus. As seen in "her bounty to the dead", humans usually lament and then forgive the sins of the dead. "Divinity" that humans pursue unlike other animals is regretfully invisible and untouchable like "shadow" and "dream". Even though Humans belong to the world on which "sun" shines, why do they feel no affection for it? Rather, why do they long for an ideal, transcendental space, alienated from the real space that they stand on? To these questions, I can answer like this: because humans would be taken after the Creator of divinity according to the Genesis of the Bible, or because they have some spiritual gene in nature, not knowing its origin like the Big Bang. They always get along with the physical things such as "sun", "fruit", "wings", "balm", and "earth", but they contradictorily feel nostalgic for some ideal space. Even though divinity is separated from humanity, the former is only significant if it should stand by the latter. It is compatible with the point that, as sinners should exist in the world, so Jesus as Saviour can exist in their mind as seen in "Divinity must live within herself". The narrator says to readers of her desirable environments and resulting feelings devoid of divinity: "rain", "snow", "blooms", "bough", four seasons accompanying several "passions", and "emotion" as the suitable conditions of her life, as shown well in "These are the measures destined for her soul." Thus, he claims greed for the earthly things can be more humanlike than they yearn for the heavenly vision.

III

Jove in the clouds had his inhuman birth.
No mother suckled him, no sweet land gave

Large-mannered motions to his mythy mind
He moved among us, as a muttering king,
Magnificent, would move among his hinds,
Until our blood, commingling, virginal,
With heaven, brought such requital to desire
The very hinds discerned it, in a star.
Shall our blood fail? Or shall it come to be
The blood of paradise? And shall the earth
Seem all of paradise that we shall know?
The sky will be much friendlier then than now,
A part of labor and a part of pain,
And next in glory to enduring love,
Not this dividing and indifferent blue.

This stanza causes us to recall W. B. Yeats' "Leda and Swan" in that it connotes the birth of religion as the result of combining divinity and humanity. By the help of chronic human abstraction, Jupiter, though being an unreal, unauthentic figure, has been recognised as if he were a real, authentic being and as if a god were projected from a mass of clay as revealed in "Jove in the clouds had his inhuman birth." Besides, what do the last four lines implicate? At first, "The sky will be much friendlier then than now" would connote Jesus' descent and ascension or would mean that humans have come to admire God. "A part of labour and a part of pain" would connote the male and female penalties or duties caused by the original sin: burden of work and baby delivery. "And next in glory to enduring love,/ Not this dividing and indifferent blue" shows us a cynical theism

insuring religion following love, which can retrieve Jesus'
maxim from our archive: Out of faith, hope and love, the
greatest of these is love (1 Cor. 13:13). If the complete
separation between heaven and humans, the situation of
"this dividing and indifferent blue", could be realised on
the earth, we would drown ourselves in a bloody ocean
that the strong reign over the weak, though it is applied
somewhat now.

IV

> She says, "I am content when wakened birds,
> Before they fly, test the reality
> Of misty fields, by their sweet questionings;
> But when the birds are gone, and their warm
> fields
> Return no more, where, then, is paradise?"
> There is not any haunt of prophecy,
> Nor any old chimera of the grave,
> Neither the golden underground, nor isle
> Melodious, where spirits gat them home,
> Nor visionary south, nor cloudy palm
> Remote on heaven's hill, that has endured
> As April's green endures; or will endure
> Like her remembrance of awakened birds,
> Or her desire for June and evening, tipped
> By the consummation of the swallow's wings.

We can't easily understand this stanza. Though, we should scan the lines because of having reason as thinking power. At first, "birds" are chirping according to instinct or nature since they were born as seen in "test the reality", though not knowing the meaning of the merry sound. And they can fly due to their innate wings. But humans can never capture the entity of "birds" by means of the symbolic net or trap like loose code. Their instinctual actions are valuable only when the narrator or humans can sense and feel them. It is natural that "birds" disappear out of human sight, behind human code and then memory or according to their instinctual, migratory direction, which can recall the theory of metaphoric "supplement" suggested by J. Derrida as the avant-garde of deconstruction. After "birds" and "springs" according to the autocratic circulation of nature fade out, where is the previous earthly "paradise"? Desperately, the narrator would say to us that we humans should recognise our transient, irreversible fate that a situation is replaced by another situation. The narrator feels futile and searches for existence alienated from "birds" as the thing itself of earth, since the "paradise" devoid of its visible, sensual entity would be meaningless.

V

> She says, "But in contentment I still feel
> The need of some imperishable bliss".
> Death is the mother of beauty; hence from her,

Alone, shall come fulfilment to our dreams
And our desires. Although she strews the leaves
Of sure obliteration on our paths,
The path sick sorrow took, the many paths
Where triumph rang its brassy phrase, or love
Whispered a little out of tenderness,
She makes the willow shiver in the sun
For maidens who were wont to sit and gaze
Upon the grass, relinquished to their feet.
She causes boys to pile new plums and pears
On disregarded plate. The maidens taste
And stray impassioned in the littering leaves.

The narrator is still pursuing the ways of immortality even on the temporary earth, which leads to not the paradise of glee but the homeostasis of death ensuring eternal peace. This world maintains peace without conflicts and with disinterestedness never allowing human blood to stir, which can be linked to the world of "nirvana", ebbing of desire. The rocking road of life spotted by of the sticky secretion of "love" and the champagne of "triumph" will have been cleared by the sweeper of "death", which shadows the present and future of energetic "willow". All humans and things on the earth will have been dominated by "death". Unconscious of the upcoming tragedy, "boys" show "maidens" "new plums and pears" to lure them for a secular fun or a sacred aim of life like reproduction. But what matters is that these fruits are put on the "disregarded plate". What does it mean? I wonder if it would mean an archaic, conventional frame or principle of life. This can be similar to the case of the newborn baby on the bed of tradition. "Maidens" gladly taste the sweet "fruits" as the baits cast by the partners, "boys", and then fall into the desolate and futile environments of life, as connoted in the "The maidens taste/ And stray impassioned in the littering leaves." Whatever ways else but this?

VI

Is there no change of death in paradise?
Does ripe fruit never fall? Or do the boughs
Hang always heavy in that perfect sky,
Unchanging, yet so like our perishing earth,
With rivers like our own that seek for seas
They never find, the same receding shores
That never touch with inarticulate pang?
Why set the pear upon those river-banks
Or spice the shores with odors of the plum?
Alas, that they should wear our colours there,
The silken weavings of our afternoons,
And pick the strings of our insipid lutes!
Death is the mother of beauty, mystical,
Within whose burning bosom we devise
Our earthly mothers waiting, sleeplessly.

This stanza shows us a few of the doubts of the afterlife. The narrator compares this gravitational, decaying life on the earth with the gravity-free, unchangeable life in paradise on the basis that our consciousness of both worlds would be the same in spite of either presence or absence of body. But this condition would be wrong. Putting off a suit of body as worn, torn, deformed and disabled clothes marching with flying age, our soul would go somewhere surely different from this world with the omnivorous body shedding blood and sweat and sense-perceiving pains. Can the conscious state of this world be guaranteed in that invisible world? I often wonder if our weary causation or human-relations on the earth would persist in the second world as seen in "Tears In Heaven", sung by the famed singer Eric Clapton: "Would you know my name/ If I saw you in heaven?/ Would it be the same/ If I saw you in heaven?"

We can guess what the strange world would be through dreams, whose functions Dr Freud suggested as condensation, displacement, and secondary elaboration. Irrespective of the rigid principles of dream, in the dream, we can disregard the physical and spiritual barriers of the tough realities surrounding us like our death forcing us to become free from debts, crimes, pains, and traps. The narrator would think of "paradise" in Christianity as the blessed space of "no change of death" where there may be un-falling "fruit", sourceless "seas", and absence of "pang". Namely, the narrator wonders if the situation of "paradise" would be similar to that of the earth. In addition, she doubts the *mise-en-scène* of things: Why does "pear" exist? Why should "plum" release "odours"? Would someone playing the "lutes" be there? For whom? But just as a slave has no idea of his master's mind, so creatures don't know the Creator's mind. Why did the Lord create the universe through the Big Bang? For whom? The key suggested by the narrator is "death" as the sacred gate of the enigmatic space while not promising the vested rights or conditions that the dead enjoyed on the earth.

In the context, Christianity denies the past states of the earth that the dead believers were faced with. But Buddhism predicts that there would happen some inequalities in the states of post-life through "Karma" as this or that causation of life on the previous earth such as reincarnations into either prince or beggar. As human monuments and masterpieces are the traces or signs practised by the entropy of "death", they get living only if they go dying every moment. The matrix for humans to start from and return to somewhere is mothers' "bosoms" as Gaia. Why were humans born on the earth? For this ultimate question, there would be three answers according to human dogmas: absurd birth or teleological mission or causational rotation. Ironically, humans imagine what "earthly mothers" would look like, though they have been embraced in their "bosoms" already.

VII

Supple and turbulent, a ring of men
Shall chant in orgy on a summer morn
Their boisterous devotion to the sun,

Not as a god, but as a god might be,
Naked among them, like a savage source.
Their chant shall be a chant of paradise,
Out of their blood, returning to the sky;
And in their chant shall enter, voice by voice,
The windy lake wherein their lord delights,
The trees, like serafin, and echoing hills,
That choir among themselves long afterward.
They shall know well the heavenly fellowship
Of men that perish and of summer morn.
And whence they came and whither they shall go
The dew upon their feet shall manifest.

Garrulous humans are chanting the hymns of their changeable, pretentious belief in pseudo-god, not the real God. Their dedications to god are caused from their inhumane purses and then head for "paradise", which is contradictory in that something secular can become something sacred offerings served to the sublime god. I doubt if God who is above materials create humans to receive the offerings. But what humans can give to the ultimate god is nothing but stale, perishable materials including money, gold, food and body as connoted in "Out of their blood, returning to the sky". The narrator doubts as to why mortal humans belong to an immortal god or invisible religion as seen in "They shall know well the heavenly fellowship/ Of men that perish and of summer morn." Humble humans try to talk to their noble god by chanting the marvellous traces of creation, such as "lake", "trees", and "hills" through their filthy, stinky mouths. In this sense, the narrator doubts the existence of God, but considerately indulges herself into empiricism as revealed in "And whence they came and whither they shall go/ The dew upon their feet shall manifest" in which experiential "dew" has the priority of life over the vacant, ideal rhetoric of religion.

VIII

> She hears, upon that water without sound,
> A voice that cries, "The tomb in Palestine
> Is not the porch of spirits lingering.
> It is the grave of Jesus, where he lay."
> We live in an old chaos of the sun,
> Or old dependency of day and night,
> Or island solitude, unsponsored, free,
> Of that wide water, inescapable.
> Deer walk upon our mountains, and the quail
> Whistle about us their spontaneous cries;
> Sweet berries ripen in the wilderness;
> And, in the isolation of the sky,
> At evening, casual flocks of pigeons make
> Ambiguous undulations as they sink,
> Downward to darkness, on extended wings.

The religious, sublime situation "upon that water without sound" invites the scene of Jesus' miraculous walking on water in the Bible. Notwithstanding, the narrator emphasises that Jesus' tomb can never be sanctified as the "Stairway to Heaven" anymore, as connoted in "The tomb in Palestine/ Is not the porch of spirits lingering./ It is the grave of Jesus, where he lay." This would mean that Jesus is not a mythic but a real figure in human history. Consequently, rather than soaring into the infinite sky like Icarus, humans must recognize that they have been surrounded with the temporary things such as "deer", "quail", "berries", and "pigeons" in the everlasting environments such as "sun", "water", "island", "mountains", "wilderness", and "sky". This would indicate the critical situation humans are faced with and they are trying to escape from the desperate space by the help of "Jesus" or alien gods.

What matters would be concerned with the last three lines: "At evening, casual flocks of pigeons make/ Ambiguous undulations as they sink,/ Downward to darkness, on extended wings." "Ambiguous undulations" cause readers to fall into the abyss of consideration. We are hanging about even though the clue would be revealed in the lines as unlettered people. Thus, I can reason that a "casual" flight of the bird having "ambiguous" direction heads for the dimension of "darkness", indicating the sinister future of the birds including all things in that their energetically "extended wings", should "sink" down someday according to the principles of gravity and entropy. Namely, the underground cells for humans to face in the future perfect tense would overshadow the "ambiguous" but ferocious struggles only for transitory survival which results in the obstinate principles, theories, dogmas, and ideologies of the genealogy of things.

Humans themselves look omniscient, transcendental, just like sages, further gods, seeing their reflections in the mirror. This would be reduced to a kind of narcissism or self-intoxication or self-misconception or fruitless masturbation. Briefly, through the flight of "pigeons", the narrator would show us the human "ambiguous" or ironical or absurd fate now flying in the abstract sky but soon scheduled to land physically.

Readers unexceptionally can become analysts with five senses capable of appreciating the text like a friend with a sweet or bitter story. Thus, we can read the next text, "The Snow Man", at your disposal irrespective of a few authoritative criticisms or views.

One must have a mind of winter
To regard the frost and the boughs
Of the pine-trees crusted with snow;

And have been cold a long time
To behold the junipers shagged with ice,
The spruces rough in the distant glitter

Of the January sun; and not to think
Of any misery in the sound of the wind,
In the sound of a few leaves,

Which is the sound of the land
Full of the same wind
That is blowing in the same bare place

For the listener, who listens in the snow,
And, nothing himself, beholds
Nothing that is not there and the nothing that is.

For humans to understand the situations of winter, can they have the wintery mind? I think that's impossible. According to the principle of semiotics, things can be recognised only by a difference of code, which F. Saussure and J. Piaget proved rationally. Thus, the human mind is incompatible with the outer environment of winter. The identification of both would be a sort of self-illusion since they maintain an arbitrary relation. Of course, I understand the narrator's sympathetic altruism to others, but both can't be united since they exist individually. So "one" can't help getting pretentious, inauthentic and egoistic, standing in the opposite direction of the wintery "pine-trees" and practising self-defence to apply him to outer, bitter, wintery situations. In detail, if we want to know what winter would be, we should have a spring mind rather than a winter mind. Similarly, to encounter Jesus, we should know that we are sinners.

The things surrounding humans are sound, including human tongues and lion's roar, and wind, such as typhoons and whirlwinds sweeping the surface of the earth. Of course, the wind has several kinds of sounds: howling or whistling. Also, wind implicates power, fashion, trend, influence, hegemony, and popularity. The two invisible elements can function as a powerful medium to transform the geography of things. They become the backgrounds of visible things which depend on them in that human sound makes people hanged and a whirl demolishes human villages. Thus, humans kill their time for their lives in grasping a truth of sound and wind and seem to hold them but in vain as if they would grip water. Similarly, "snow man", "nothing" as temporarily frozen crystals of water, seems to exist in our sight, but soon is melted and disappeared like a phantom as if it were absent there, which would implicate the narrator's strong doubt of existence and reality as its reflection on the earth.

Reading "The Idea of Order at Key West", readers may feel perplexed because of the cryptic resistant gestures of its modernism. But the poem can't help being signified into our loose tongues this or that. Thus, we should give up a complete comprehension of things or a poem since the distance between things and code as their medium is too far. In this sense, as you like it, the virtuoso of the minor note, F. Schubert's "Unfinished Symphony", is not unfinished but finished. Consequently, readers can use either "misreading", as suggested by H. Bloom, or close reading according to each taste to touch this esoteric poem since neither can be the absolute means to read the poem.

She sang beyond the genius of the sea.
The water never formed to mind or voice,
Like a body wholly body, fluttering
its empty sleeves; and yet its mimic motion
Made constant cry, caused constantly a cry,
That was not ours although we understood,
Inhuman, of the veritable ocean.

Readers may think of the blue but white sea, like the teeth of a shark of "Key West", in Florida. Here "she" and "sea" suddenly emerge. At the seashore, "she" is singing, but she can't be united into one body, since she and sea are intersubjective. The girl is singing according to her will and the sea is splashing and roaring according to the law of nature. The relation between the girl and sea collapses as the former is influenced by the latter, but the latter can't fill the former with wind or anything else as connoted in "empty sleeves". "Mimic motion" and the roll of wave means the repetition of a natural phenomenon completely irrespective of the human will. Although the girl listens to the sound, it belongs to the sea, not to her. "Sea" and wave never circulate for humans' sake and are alienated from the human will. "Sea" will run opposite to humans that would regard the water as his property until the end of the world.

> The sea was not a mask. No more was she.
> The song and water were not medleyed sound
> Even if what she sang was what she heard,
> Since what she sang was uttered word by word.
> It may be that in all her phrases stirred
> The grinding water and the gasping wind;
> But it was she and not the sea we heard.

Her "song" is arbitrary or self-referential unconcerned with nature or "sea" as connoted in "The sea was not a mask. No more was she". Here "sea" would mean the thing itself alienated from her description or articulation. Thus her "song" and "water" remain separated in that the "song" doesn't correspond to "water" but to the articulated, syntactical system out of her consciousness. We can never listen to the "song" of "sea" with ears blocked by earphones or contaminated by human grammar or self-contained thinking but her "song" fit for human convention. Code or language or the discourse of the other pre-exists in her mind so that she can hear the merely distorted song of "sea" via her consciousness full of cultural thoughts as revealed in "But it was she and not the sea we heard."

> For she was the maker of the song she sang.
> The ever-hooded, tragic-gestured sea
> Was merely a place by which she walked to sing.
> Whose spirit is this? we said, because we knew
> It was the spirit that we sought and knew
> That we should ask this often as she sang.

She is singing a song made by herself at the seashore as an element of nature. Here happens some *mise-en-scène* composed of "she", "song", "sea", and "we" as the community of convention. What is the entity of spirit composing the "song" that "we knew" already? The "song" will be inherited forever since "we should ask" it frequently only if the human community will remain on the earth. The "spirit" lurking behind the "song" reminds me of F. Hegel's "the Absolute Idealism" to reign over all things and drive individuals as parts subject to the sublime spirit that heads for the perfection of self with which all parts should cooperate. Simultaneously, I. Kant is invited in our sights. We can focus on his idea as "Copernican revolution", but we can't recognise thing itself, and our cognition can make its concept. Namely, humans can't know a thing itself as a bare thing but can know its concept as a thing wrapped in thought or tongue. Accordingly, Kant argued that truth is not far away beyond human sight but exists in human hands or mind, since we can judge the truth reasoned in our process of thought in time and space as the "*a priori* (pre-experience) intuition" as the scene where we undergo diverse experiences, which are called "apriorism". Finally, she is alienated from the real "sea" since she lingers around the "sea" of mind.

> If it was only the dark voice of the sea
> That rose, or even coloured by many waves;
> If it was only the outer voice of sky
> And cloud, of the sunken coral water-walled,
> However clear, it would have been deep air,
> The heaving speech of air, a summer sound
> Repeated in a summer without end
> And sound alone. But it was more than that,/

Readers can see the arrangement of all things, namely the backgrounds of nature, whose intention nobody knows still. The situation is not signified into technical terms but ambiguously referred to "sound" and "colour", which would mean the revelation or epiphany of presence, not tinted by linguistic MSG (monosodium glutamate). The sound of the sea, the sky as a tongue of the air, summer pre-exists and overcomes humans' temporary and local sound. Further, this reminds me of "The sublime" suggested by Jean-Francois Lyotard, which happens when humans often encounter speechless elements or agape situations free from their syntactic system.

> More even than her voice, and ours, among
> The meaningless plungings of water and the wind,
> Theatrical distances, bronze shadows heaped
> On high horizons, mountainous atmospheres
> Of sky and sea.

The awesome spectacle spreading before the narrator's sight causes us to generate a sublime feeling, which s/he would forget for a while since s/he has been indulged into a self-contained situation or narcissism. This can't help getting alienated from human signification system as revealed in "The meaningless plungings of water and the wind".

> It was her voice that made
> The sky acutest at its vanishing.
> She measured to the hour its solitude.
> She was the single artificer of the world
> In which she sang. And when she sang, the sea,

Human voices used to ring the sky as if they could understand its solitude within their lives, though in vain. Like this, "she" becomes the sole inventor that can

represent all things on earth and should sing the worldly
songs irrespective of the world.

> Whatever self it had, became the self
> That was her song, for she was the maker. Then we,
> As we beheld her striding there alone,
> Knew that there was never a world for her
> Except the one she sang and, singing, made.

The meaningless, random sea has been personified
and has gone as far as to become a god, Neptune, as
revealed in "became the self". Thus sea can gulp humans
and capsize their ships. But the sea is running on its way
now according to the laws of nature. Sea, deaf to her
mournful song, is indifferent to the victims and damages,
having the immanent will. Sea and humans run on each
opposite track as denoted in "As we beheld her striding
there alone". The world where she is living is not the one
the Creator created for her but the one she herself made,
as seen in the movie *The Truman Show*, which reminds
me of the Kantian view or phenomenal view in that she
can see the sea in her mind, incapable of seeing the sea
itself as connoted in "there was never a world for her/
Except the one she sang and, singing, made."

> Ramon Fernandez, tell me, if you know,
> Why, when the singing ended and we turned
> Toward the town, tell why the glassy lights,
> The lights in the fishing boats at anchor there,

As the night descended, tilting in the air,
Mastered the night and portioned out the sea,
Fixing emblazoned zones and fiery poles,
Arranging, deepening, enchanting night.

"Ramon" with a brighter insight for things is inquired. What does "when the singing ended and we turned/ Toward the town" connote? Many scholars of poetry may wander around this line here and there. But the right interpretation is absent since we live in the fake world according to Plato's Idea. Notwithstanding, we can't give up the production of its meanings. I dare to think of it, humans are intoxicated by some inauthentic principles, like her "singing", for a while, but accidentally they come to think of the origin of existence like "town" for their matrix, which would mean a kind of nostalgic feeling toward some authentic truth. Accordingly, the following lines would mean that "light" grows encroaching dark, borderless "night" whose boundary gets more apparent as implicated in "portioned out" "the sea" of the "night". The narrator asks "Ramon" what the reason is or in other words why the enlightenment of "light" should reign over the darkness of "night". The narrator would doubt the reason for establishing the boundary between "light" and "night". "Light", as the "anchor" of life, overshadows "night" and builds a magnificent "pole" of life like carbon dioxide assimilation and brilliant "zones" like Hollywood or Las Vegas, but both maintain complementary relations, since "light" functions as the essential element to brighten and beautify "night".

Oh! Blessed rage for order, pale Ramon,
The maker's rage to order words of sea
Words of the fragrant portals, dimly-starred,
And of ourselves and our origins,
In ghostlier demarcations, keener sounds.

The structure of the earth separated from humans is disregarded by most of the people, including animals loyal to eating and then reproducing blind to the cause of Genesis. Many common people live joyful lives with bluffing and flush, while a few sensible people, including A. Camus and F. Kafka, live the tragic lives full of unbearable agony, like Jesus nailed on the thorny cross for the sake of all sinners. "Pale Ramon" would belong to the latter category. The world would be similar to the grand Coliseum, where diverse lines of gladiators stand against each other. In the battles of election, business and examination, some survive but others die, which is the command of nature. The famed critic, "Ramon", would be the blessed person to sense the thrilling structure of things as sensed in "Blessed rage for order", but the others would be those cursed since they have no idea of it. The anger of "The maker" would be represented through "the words of sea" rather than the noisy words of humans. The sacred tongue would lead humans to the portals of agnosticism so that the narrator could experience a kind of epiphany through "the words of sea" in the confusing, dreamy mentality as revealed "In ghostlier demarcations, keener sounds".

CHAPTER 9

DYLAN THOMAS: REFUSAL OF GENERALIZATION

When you think of Dylan Thomas, what do you retrieve? The fact that the famed singer Bob Dylan is named after him? Or that the poet pursued vitality rather than nihilistic weakness, helplessness, and defeatism? Additionally, a tint of Nietzschean idea proclaiming "the death of God" and "the birth of Superman" can be revealed in that he derided human mortality and resisted theology. He refused the transcendental views of life and searched for the realistic stances favouring even a temporary life. He hated the futility that short, invaluable time given to humans must be spent in metaphysical or platonic agony.

It is said that he indulged himself in reading D. H. Lawrence's works, which also would affect his works favouring and admiring nature. Wonderfully, most of his poems were written in his teens, which proved that would-be poets should write their poems in the purest period. But one of the main causes of what shortened the poet's lifespan was alcohol rather than opium, tuberculosis or womanising as is the case with most noted poets. His dynamic lyrics and fiery passion remind us of the stereotyped poems of romanticism. He lived a poet-like life, which included the flamboyant affairs: multiple love-affairs and participation as an anti-aircraft gunner instead of as a penman in World War II. Risking much criticism from a community loyal to externalism, he spontaneously fell in love with an acquaintance's mistress and even married her. What is more impressive, like most wandering minstrels in the ancient times, he recited his poems in public across America as if firmly holding the banner of logocentrism securing the presence of the poet.

Now, read his notorious poem, "Do not go gentle into that good night", which reminds us of obstinate resistance to destiny and strong will of life and the solid gesture of an activist resisting a dictatorship. Additionally, this poem was introduced in the scientific movie *Interstellar*, showing us the apocalyptic situation in which most humans on earth perished due to eccentric, unusual weather and a few people strived to find the novel way of survival off the earth.

> Do not go gentle into that good night,
> Old age should burn and rave at close of day;
> Rage, rage against the dying of the light.

This part reminds us of "old age" lying down in some care hospitals. Losing youth, they are living a hard life resorting to nurses or volunteers, which will have foreshadowed the narrator's future. But the poet died of over-drinking in his thirties and thereby avoided death from ageing, not knowing the sorrow of ageing. The narrator resists the stereotyped, general recognition of naturally accepting ageing, when he/she becomes old. This would be similar to a Nietzschean thought like the spirit of Superman to wrestle with a kind of Sisyphus' fate. Or it would be a post-human idea of anti-ageing to reduce the velocity of death to devour humans.

> Though wise men at their end know dark is right,
> Because their words had forked no lightning they
> Do not go gentle into that good night.

This part would be concerned with Buddhism in that it indifferently deals with death like a criminal who volunteered to make himself/herself chained. Thus, the transcendental dogma or recognition of life suggested by oriental or occidental "wise men" such as Buddha and Socrates may sound rather empty to the narrator.

> Good men, the last wave by, crying how bright
> Their frail deeds might have danced in a green bay,
> Rage, rage against the dying of the light.

There have been no sinners in the world since they weren't born for themselves but the Other would exist as their Creator. That's all right? Is there anyone to create himself on the earth? In this sense, the Nietzschean resistance to Christianity's view of all humans as sinners even before their birth is plausible. But when it should be recognized that we as fragile, aging pottery are weaker than the omniscient potter as Creator, as there are few appropriate ways to the afterlife in the realities, we can't help choosing Christianity and believing in Jesus who proclaimed himself the sole road, truth, and life in the journey to heaven. Humans, intelligent or illiterate, never know the authentic purpose of the creation of the universe or big bang, only guessing it in this or that way. Thus, Western existentialists lamented for this desperate situation and felt appalled like the anonymous human shocked in Edward Munch's painting "The Scream". Accordingly, the narrator would point to the helplessness that humans have no comfort at all, burdened with the mechanism of oppression of death in advance. Despite the destiny that as long as we breathe, we must live to the end, we never enjoy our days obsessed with the fear of death.

> Wild men who caught and sang the sun in flight,
> And learn, too late, they grieved it on its way,
> Do not go gentle into that good night.

Originally, humans are "wild" and naked. But they wear some clothes of culture for themselves. Furthermore, they are castrated by culture or narcissism or self-intoxication and reborn into the transcendental creations, so-called the birth of holy humans pretending to reign over nature such as the Egyptian Pharaoh and the Inca emperors. Notwithstanding this human "wild" brag, it is foolish for humans to grasp the sun and worship it since both should each run on a different track. Humans tend to interpret sublime nature in their views as if we think the moon would shine only on us. But the planet remains neutral and indifferent to our selfish, "wild" will. Even after the Chinese emperor Shi, the Egyptian Pharaohs, and the Inca emperors, seemingly eternal beings, passed away, the sun remains intact over us. Also, after we will have passed away, the sun must run its own orbit until the end of the universe, which reminds us of the maxim of "The Future Lasts Forever", suggested by the famed French famed sociologist Louis Althusser.

> Grave men, near death, who see with blinding sight
> Blind eyes could blaze like meteors and be gay,
> Rage, rage against the dying of the light.

Even the "grave men" should enjoy their lives, though they are getting old and "blind" and approaching the black-out of death. But just before entering the irreversible gate, you should enjoy your lives as much as you can. This reminds me of the Korean maxim like "Although humans would bog down in the mire of the earth, they had better live on the earth rather than stay in boring heaven." The narrator urges us not to give up our lives in advance, though we would face even fatal catastrophes. Both life and death are equally given to humans poor or rich, low or high, possessing the fate of passing but burning "meteors".

And you, my father, there on the sad height,
Curse, bless, me now with your fierce tears, I pray.
Do not go gentle into that good night.
Rage, rage against the dying of the light.

Father in Heaven! Why do you curse and bless humans? You loved some people much more, while you severely cursed other people in the Bible. Why can't you, as the Absolute, love everybody? But humans as humble creations have no idea of your sacred intentions of Genesis. In this sense, the narrator resists God's will and plot as if he were a Prometheus that eagles might peck at his liver even in a live state, or a Sisyphus incessantly pushing a round stone up to the hill finally to roll it down, or a Samson turning a millstone of painful realities. Accordingly, we should resist the generalisation of "good night" domesticating humans into the tailored convention of sleeping as a kind of extinction despite having the double meanings.

In the next poem, "And Death Shall Have No Dominion", resistance to death is revealed apparently with a glimpse. But the death that the narrator resists is relative, contrary to life but rather complementary with it. So both keep pace with the inseparable relation of twins with different faces in the same womb.

And death shall have no dominion.
Dead men naked they shall be one
With the man in the wind and the west moon;

When their bones are picked clean and the clean
bones gone,
They shall have stars at elbow and foot;
Though they go mad they shall be sane,
Though they sink through the sea they shall rise
again;
Though lovers be lost love shall not;
And death shall have no dominion.

This stanza triggers us to think of the essence
of Things which would be composed of six elements
in Buddhism—material section: earth (matrix of
generating) /water (liquid of growing) /fire (energy of
maturing) /wind (movement of transformation); abstract
section: distance (gap between things) /knowledge
(recognizing things), among which the former was
recognized by the Greek philosopher, Empedocles. The
Buddhist idea is similar to Western dualism (mind/
body). Unlike the resistance to death, this poem would
lead us to some optimism beyond life, proclaiming
that death can't be horror to humans who would be
transformed into nature after life rather than the slaves
of death.

And death shall have no dominion.
Under the windings of the sea
They lying long shall not die windily;
Twisting on racks when sinews give way,
Strapped to a wheel, yet they shall not break;

Faith in their hands shall snap in two,
And the unicorn evils run them through;
Split all ends up they shan't crack;
And death shall have no dominion.

Humans seem to die, but they never die since they remain in other forms after life, which can be called "the principle of mass conservation" or culturally the principle of otherness, meaning that we should be subject to others and vice versa. In Christianity, they shall rise up when Jesus comes here again from Heaven. Nonetheless, what humans should recognise is that they are attacked within and without, spiritually and physically for their lifespan. The narrator would stress that death in the view of humans is never death in the view of nature, so nature never minds death as death becomes the motive of birth. Consequently, after life, we shall have been reduced to other things without death, of course, contrary to Christianity.

And death shall have no dominion.
No more may gulls cry at their ears
Or waves break loud on the seashore;
Where blew a flower may a flower no more
Lift its head to the blows of the rain;
Through they be mad and dead as nails,
Heads of the characters hammer through daisies;
Break in the sun till the sun breaks down,
And death shall have no dominion.

The narrator's argument is not unreasonable in that humans as nature itself never die. Have readers ever seen nature completely pass away? Hence humans with the invincible force of nature can hammer even "the sun" to extinction someday. Namely, as they are a mass or a member of nature, their immortal lives, rather employing death, survive any over-scaring death, which connotes the best core of the sutra of Buddhism or Upanishad of Hinduism viewing life and death as the same thing. Finally, humans as nature never die and are only being transformed into other things despite the narrator's feeble outcry of "death shall have no dominion".

CHAPTER 10

BOB DYLAN:
PRACTICE OF THE FRANKFORT SCHOOL

Readers, let's think of Bob Dylan (henceforth, Bob). At first, you can retrieve "Beat Generation" in the 1960s. He was in the company of hairy, cute Joan Baez in his twenties. Now, even in his seventies, he favours recitals roaming here and there across America, like the minstrels in the middle black age of the continent, pursuing the presence of the poet like the shaman of logocentrism. He himself composed and sang many lyrics about not abstract but sanguine and vivid realities. But readers can't dispel their doubts as to whether he would be an authentic poet. In the meanwhile, many people can't help but recognise his capacity as a poet after he recently received the Nobel Prize for literature, beating numerous writers worldwide, such as the Japanese Murakami Haruki, who had won other prestigious prizes in literature.

Of course, some works of literature can't resort to competitions or be measured by a few of critics because of political tricks that apparently reside in the human society. In my thought, the reason Bob won the prize may be due to his passionate participation in the tough realities and encouragement of those in desperation to rise up through his specifically cynical, sarcastic, humane positions on the issues of life. Perhaps, he may resemble Lord George Byron. At first, as we read "One More Cup of Coffee", we can feel Bob's inclination toward some ideal, a little, even if not completely.

> Your breath is sweet
> Your eyes are like two jewels in the sky
> Your back is straight your hair is smooth
> On the pillow where you lie
> But I don't sense affection
> No gratitude or love
> Your loyalty is not to me
> But to the stars above
>
> One more cup of coffee for the road
> One more cup of coffee 'fore I go.
> To the valley below.

This stanza shows us the aspect of concreteness ruling over abstractness. Namely, physical elements such as "breath", "eyes", and "back" are credited more, while "affection", "love", "gratitude", and "loyalty" are discredited more just as words without actions are futile, helpless to us, and Macbeth, loyal to the king, murdered him. In the meantime, humans, like a spectrum radiating diverse colours, become the source, producing the colourful meanings of things related to and surrounding them. They have a stronger tendency to approach strange things rather than familiar things on which their sights temporarily stay. In "the valley below", due to the differences of meanings or ideologies, ferocious battles are happening now, taken or taking. To this inevitable, apocalyptic situation, humans don't need to dash hurriedly. Rather we should have some room to take "One more cup of coffee", which would be a wise choice for a better life. Namely, the narrator would urge us to restore the vitality of kairos rather than falling down into the deterministic chronos of life. Do humans dying every day need to die in haste?

> Your daddy he's an outlaw
> And a wanderer by trade
> He'll teach you how to pick and choose
> And how to throw the blade
> He oversees his kingdom
> So no stranger does intrude
> His voice it trembles as he calls out
> For another plate of food.
>
> One more cup of coffee for the road
> One more cup of coffee 'fore I go.
> To the valley below.

Here the ways of life are suggested, which never secures the comfortable area and invite verbal quarrels and tough wrestles. This reminds us of the Roman Coliseum, in which numerous, innocent gladiators fought each other and passed away like the morning dew for the Romans' attractions. Regretfully, this world, I think, is the sphere of entropy to slaughter others for our own survival, according to the guidance or taste of the Creator as the only spectator. So don't ask why humans should die sooner or later, which would be the sacred providence or command of the First Cause either to love them or to hate them. God may now see the oppositional spectacles in which I or Europeans or Americans have a hamburger greedily despite the skinny African children crying in hunger on TV.

Additionally, God has presented humans with the inner ghosts called conflict or agony, so they should defeat both inner and outer foes or be perished as seen in "And how to throw the blade/ He oversees his kingdom". Facing these sanguine realities, we as egoists always long for the victorious realities. As connoted in "His voice it trembles as he calls out/ For another plate of food", we should consider the two dimensions, economical and biological, for a normalised life. The former part collides with the latter in that when a man is lured by a street girl, the mating should cost him the living expenses of one week in return for momentary, instinctual pleasure. Thus, the man's voice desiring instinctual pleasure can't help but shake, bumped against the economic realities.

Your sister sees the future
Like your mama and yourself
You've never learned to read or write
There's no books upon your shelf

And your pleasure knows no limits
Your voice is like a meadowlark
But your heart is like an ocean
Mysterious and dark.

One more cup of coffee for the road
One more cup of coffee 'fore I go.
To the valley below.

This stanza shows us the meanings of literacy and illiteracy. Mostly, humans generally prefer the former to the latter, but the narrator unexpectedly chooses the opposite. This is similar to the Oriental view to be wary of letters as the barriers to prevent us from reaching presence or things. He would urge us to have a room capable of drinking "one more cup of coffee", not giving up even a "cup of coffee" because of haunted daily affairs. To drink a cup of coffee, which seems to be an existential performance, would be worthy of a trial to restore himself.

The next poem to read is "Blowin' in the Wind", which has aired across the world every day.

How many roads must a man walk down
Before you call him a man?
How many seas must a white dove sail
Before she sleeps in the sand?
Yes, and how many times must the cannon balls fly
Before they're forever banned?

The answer, my friend, is blowin' in the wind
The answer is blowin' in the wind.

For babies to become a male, they should go through the socialisation, normalisation, and castration as some processes to domesticate their wild desire. To achieve this state, humans should undergo several rites of individuation as the steps of adaptation for an organisation like a curriculum of a college. Namely, the community would prefer an essential male wearing a uniform to an existential male favouring independence. The former as an inauthentic being is signified in the society, while the latter as an authentic being is immutable. Thus, the narrator would reflect this regretful situation. But to adapt to society, we should wear the mask of essence stipulated for its maintenance. Here "essence" is not innate but designed and plotted by humans.

In this sense, I agree with J. P. Sartre's maxim that "existence precedes essence". For another theme, the relief of the "dove", which would be a human-centred idea, apparently resorts to the immanent will of nature according to its free will or instinct. Accordingly, refusing human concern, it comforts itself irrespective of human interruption or will according to the surroundings. It is why the relationship between humans and "dove" is that of an "epistemological break". The last theme would be concerned with human essence. Speaking of it in advance, "cannon balls" never disappear from the earth because they become the motives of construction and destruction as the main missions of humans in a lifetime. The bombs invented by A. Nobel are flying over our heads, digging deep furrows to sow the seeds of construction and being contributed to the decrease in population density.

Of course, I deeply understand the narrator's humanitarianism in criticising the ferocity of bombs, but if double-bladed bombs disappear from the earth, humans will lose the goal of life to dominate and rule over others, living boring and monotonous lives, especially the avaricious dictators of powers. Thus, "bombs" would be the presents descending from heaven and giving them their thrill and interest in life, like landed Jesus to save sinful humans. Finally, humans can prove their sacred or secular identity through the play or game of the firecracker.

> Yes, and how many years can a mountain exist
> Before it is washed to the sea?
> Yes, and how many years can some people exist
> Before they're allowed to be free?
> Yes, and how many times can a man turn his head
> And pretend that he just doesn't see?
>
> The answer, my friend, is blowin' in the wind
> The answer is blowin' in the wind.

According to radiocarbon dating, the age of the earth would amount to around 4.6 billion years. Naturally, "mountain" is being eroded by weather and will finally have been transformed into ground or sea before human sense. The loss of the "mountain" in which many cowboys and outlaws used to fight with guns at the risk of their lives means that of human history. This reminds us of the Chinese maxim "Convulsions of nature" (A mulberry field has been transformed into a sea). In this sense, by the immanent will of nature, mountains become sea and vice versa as shown in the sea fossils of deep mountains.

The irreversible power may belong to the Superman in the movies, or transcendental religions like Christianity have the miracle that the Red Sea might be divided. For another theme, humans are the existences far from absolute freedom. To enjoy freedom, they should confine themselves to the democratic system or should live in slavery like the North Koreans under communism. The time to take to gain freedom would be proportional to the level of democracy. For the last theme, the narrator reflects on inhumanity or indifference for human affairs like overlooking the hungry, skinny African children on the TV and the miserable North Koreans crossing the rapid of the border at the risk of their lives.

> Yes, and how many times must a man look up
> Before he can see the sky?
> Yes, and how many ears must one man have
> Before he can hear people cry?
> Yes, and how many deaths will it take 'til he knows
> That too many people have died?
>
> The answer, my friend, is blowin' in the wind
> The answer is blowin' in the wind.

Humans as earthly creatures creeping over the land never "look up" but look down to the ground in search of feed or prey. Those who truly "can see the sky" like a Buddha overcoming life and death would be few. If the majority of humans on earth remain good and generous, it will become a paradise that communism would pursue, though lions don't get together with humans in the same cage. For another theme, of course, although they themselves groan with pains from their thorny and bitter realities, humans should hear others' screams and sympathise with them.

For the last theme, we shouldn't overlook others' deaths as if they would be neighbours or strangers as revealed well in John Donne's lines of "For whom the bell tolls?": "No man is an island,/ Entire of itself,/ Every man is a piece of the continent,/ A part of the main./ If a clod be washed away by the sea,/ Europe is the less." Anyhow, the right answer to the overwhelming, ultimate questions can be reduced to the "wind" as the Creator's breath, though acataleptic. The feathery breeze born from China would fly across the Pacific and be changed into the terrible "wind", tornado devouring even trailer-trucks in America according to the owner's command. In this sense, the narrator that puts the secrets of things at the disposal of the "wind" as nature would communicate with the Chinese Taoist, Lao-tzu.

CONCLUSION

A DYSTOPIAN/UTOPIAN PERSPECTIVE OF POETRY

Readers, I introduce a poem by a Korean poet, Kim Chun-soo. This poem, titled "Flowers" in Korean, can't be completely translated into English. It is why things should be changed into code (signifier plus signified) to show them up to humans, when the former has arbitrary relation with the latter. Tree, as something physical, is represented in several tongues, such as English, French, German, and Korean, as something abstract. Hence, this case reminds us of the Buddhist maxim: "When people want to see the moon, rather they strive to see only the finger pointing to her." Humans look at the abstract things as letters rather than the physical things as concrete objects, so they naturally become alienated from the real things. Likewise, this translation can't help being far from the poem itself, which can prove Ludwig Wittgenstein's "language game" naming things in human society.

Before calling her name
she had been nothing but a gesture.
When I uttered her name,
she came closer to me and became a flower.
This time call my name too,
fit for my colour and scent,
as just as I had called hers
So that I may access her and become her flower.
We all long for becoming something.
I want to become an unforgettable meaning for you
And vice versa.

Readers, would you guess the theme? This poem reminds us of Saussure's linguistic principle: a code is composed of both a signifier (word or image or pronunciation) and the signifieds (meanings). Thus, flowers in a mountain, if not having their names, never exist in the human community. Likewise, humans can't become individuals if not possessing their names, which would mean the birth of a linguistic subject. Of course, besides my interpretation, other views to the poem can be possible. With the advent of the postmodern era, it is said that authors have died and readers have been born, a position seconded earlier by M. Foucault and R. Barthes.

In the Black Age of the spreading pest, poets like a Nostradamus foretold the future as a shaman. From the Enlightenment Era, through Romanticism and Realism, until Modernism, they tried to deviate from or reflect the then cruel realities of survival, and today poets fed up with the given tools of rhetoric are indulged in avant-garde trends for "art for art's sake", though prevalent in 1830s, favouring the fun of the tongue rather than the pursuit of truth. In the meantime, especially I am interested in imagism, starting in the early twenty-first century from both England and America, "objective correlative" suggested by T. S. Eliot as another term concerned with imagism, and symbolism, spanning the long term of eighteenth to twentieth centuries in Europe. What is more apparent is for humans not to reach the shore of truth, since they can touch things through the medium of the tongue and they can't refer to each other. Although there is no truth on the earth, they have only the tongue as the means of truth, through which humans cry out, "Look at truth!"

Thus I can second Macbeth's confession: "To-morrow, and to-morrow, and to-morrow,/ Creeps in this petty pace from day to day,/ To the last syllable of recorded time;/ And all our yesterdays have lighted fools/ The way to dusty death. Out, out, brief candle!/ Life's but a walking shadow, a poor player/ That struts and frets his hour upon the stage/ And then is heard no more. It is a tale/ Told by an idiot, full of sound and fury/ Signifying nothing." The last line "Signifying nothing" would be impressive since, even though we remark each opinion of something, it is really meaningless, because our democratic opinions are divergent and things and tongues are arbitrary to each other.

If so, what is the reason for the existence of poetry? Postmodernism has slaughtered the mystery of poetry as the core with waving the banner of populism. Thus, everybody can write poems and non-critics can criticise them in their views, which can be called the death of the poet and the birth of the public. The collections of poems replaced the poets and digital devices have replaced the pulp texts. The poets hid behind the books, but the digital media have made the dead poets revive like Jesus. The late poet T. S. Eliot is now reciting his famed poem "The Waste Land", specifically looking serious. The main reason serious poets and readers have been disappearing would arise from the advent of the electronic era, which trusts human intelligence to computer or AI (artificial intelligence). Thus, contemporary people don't write poems, except a few professional poets and class students, but are absorbed in playing electronic games with alien monsters, simulacra, reproduced by cyberspace. Of course, the classical penchant for poetry will survive even in future, though not on a wide scale, as archaeology is still studied in the postmodern era in favour of synchronism, and classical music in the digital era is now pursued by a few enthusiasts in Asia but has a lot of fans in Europe.

The so-called post-humanism, meaning the combination or convergence between human and machine, is surging like a mountainous tide and changing human mind and body into a kind of cyborg. This would not be a strange phenomenon since humans resorted to extraneous machinery such as hammer, spear, spoon, fork, knife, chariot, steam train, bicycle, and eyeglasses several hundred years earlier. Conversely, this time the machinery is being permeated and embedded into the human mind and body as inner devices such as artificial organs and intelligence replacing the functions of the heart and brain. Thus, machinery has perfectly reigned over humans composed of outer and inner parts, which M. McLuhan, the late forerunner of medium, called the "extension" of medium. Accordingly, the alien and odd beings staged in the series of the scientific movies, like *Transformers* or *The Terminator*, as mechanical beings can't be imaginary or fictional beings afterward. In this sense, intelligent and physical humans depending on machinery can't help but grow gradually weaker.

A deeper speculation on some change of the universe will be scarce except for a few professionals and technocrats studying the interface between human and machine because humans unconsciously enjoy the merits and benefits of machinery to work or deputise for them. Namely, the humans of the twenty-first century will enjoy the great pleasures of immense and recreational thinking, as their life will become freer due to the untiring proliferation of technology and mechanical servants. In this comfortable, happy situation, the post-humans who hate complicated thinking and get accustomed to passive thinking will not try to write a dizzy, complicated poem. Those pursuing the pleasure of the surface such as computer games will have no time to speculate on serious, esoteric poetry. Perhaps to prevent human headache caused by writing poems, writing robot will write poems and bring them to humans. If so, will poetry lose its pride of status acquired over centuries in the electronic future of the twenty-first century? I don't think so, though I'm scared of the possibility. Poetry will sustain its life since the human community is composed of codes, and poetry and its by-products are made up of codes.

As the Nobel Prize winner in literature, Bob Dylan, is still writing lyrics and singing them to console all of the people in the world, and in the less democratic era of the past, soul lyrics written by anonymous singers and sung like talking, comforted black humans in the tough labour of slavery, thus the poetry of the future will remain in some forms of hyper-real means, not knowing whatever media may be mobilized, and cheer humans who are in the distress of digital environments indulging themselves in more strange situations caused by the Fourth Industrial Revolution perhaps leading to the end of history, since if poetry perishes, it would mean the extinction of humanity as if it collided with a comet.

The end

Printed in the United States
By Bookmasters